FINANCIAL RATIOS FOR EXECUTIVES

HOW TO ASSESS COMPANY STRENGTH, FIX PROBLEMS, AND MAKE BETTER DECISIONS

Michael Rist

Albert J. Pizzica

Apress®

Financial Ratios for Executives: How to Assess Company Strength, Fix Problems, and Make Better Decisions

ISBN-13 (pbk): 978-1-4842-0732-1

ISBN-13 (electronic): 978-1-4842-0731-4

Trademarked names, logos, and images may appear in this book. Rather than use a trademark symbol with every occurrence of a trademarked name, logo, or image we use the names, logos, and images only in an editorial fashion and to the benefit of the trademark owner, with no intention of infringement of the trademark.

The use in this publication of trade names, trademarks, service marks, and similar terms, even if they are not identified as such, is not to be taken as an expression of opinion as to whether or not they are subject to proprietary rights.

While the advice and information in this book are believed to be true and accurate at the date of publication, neither the authors nor the editors nor the publisher can accept any legal responsibility for any errors or omissions that may be made. The publisher makes no warranty, express or implied, with respect to the material contained herein.

Managing Director: Welmoed Spahr
Acquisitions Editor: Jeff Olson
Editorial Board: Steve Anglin, Mark Beckner, Gary Cornell, Louise Corrigan, James DeWolf,
  Jonathan Gennick, Robert Hutchinson, Michelle Lowman, James Markham,
  Matthew Moodie, Jeff Olson, Jeffrey Pepper, Douglas Pundick, Ben Renow-Clarke,
  Gwenan Spearing, Matt Wade, Steve Weiss
Coordinating Editor: Rita Fernando
Copy Editor: Laura Lawrie
Compositor: SPi Global
Indexer: SPi Global
Cover Designer: Mila Perry

Distributed to the book trade worldwide by Springer Science+Business Media New York, 233 Spring Street, 6th Floor, New York, NY 10013. Phone 1-800-SPRINGER, fax (201) 348-4505, e-mail orders-ny@springer-sbm.com, or visit www.springeronline.com. Apress Media, LLC is a California LLC and the sole member (owner) is Springer Science + Business Media Finance Inc (SSBM Finance Inc). SSBM Finance Inc is a **Delaware** corporation.

For information on translations, please e-mail rights@apress.com, or visit www.apress.com.

Apress and friends of ED books may be purchased in bulk for academic, corporate, or promotional use. eBook versions and licenses are also available for most titles. For more information, reference our Special Bulk Sales–eBook Licensing web page at www.apress.com/bulk-sales.

Any source code or other supplementary materials referenced by the author in this text is available to readers at www.apress.com. For detailed information about how to locate your book's source code, go to www.apress.com/source-code/.

Apress Business: The Unbiased Source of Business Information

Apress business books provide essential information and practical advice, each written for practitioners by recognized experts. Busy managers and professionals in all areas of the business world—and at all levels of technical sophistication—look to our books for the actionable ideas and tools they need to solve problems, update and enhance their professional skills, make their work lives easier, and capitalize on opportunity.

Whatever the topic on the business spectrum—entrepreneurship, finance, sales, marketing, management, regulation, information technology, among others—Apress has been praised for providing the objective information and unbiased advice you need to excel in your daily work life. Our authors have no axes to grind; they understand they have one job only—to deliver up-to-date, accurate information simply, concisely, and with deep insight that addresses the real needs of our readers.

It is increasingly hard to find information—whether in the news media, on the Internet, and now all too often in books—that is even-handed and has your best interests at heart. We therefore hope that you enjoy this book, which has been carefully crafted to meet our standards of quality and unbiased coverage.

We are always interested in your feedback or ideas for new titles. Perhaps you'd even like to write a book yourself. Whatever the case, reach out to us at editorial@apress.com and an editor will respond swiftly. Incidentally, at the back of this book, you will find a list of useful related titles. Please visit us at www.apress.com to sign up for newsletters and discounts on future purchases.

The Apress Business Team

Contents

About the Authors

Michael Rist is a senior financial executive with more than 20 years of international operations and business experience within corporate finance for public and privately-held companies and Big 4 public accounting. He has previously been chief financial officer of Mosaica Education, Inc., The Elwing Company, and SES Engineering. He has worked across the telecommunication, technology, pharmaceutical, industrial manufacturing, and education industries. He is a Certified Public Accountant and active in a number of professional organizations. Rist holds a BS in Accounting and Finance from Copenhagen Business School and an MBA from the School of Business, Villanova University.

Albert J. Pizzica is an entrepreneur with experience at half a dozen startup companies. He is currently Vice President of Strategic Programs at American Aerospace and Vice President of Government and Defense Programs at The Elwing Company. He is also the principal at Pizzica Industries LLC, a startup and medium business consulting company. Pizzica's previous experience includes aseptic vaccine manufacturing operations at Merck and as a U.S. Navy officer in various operations roles. Pizzica holds a BS in Mechanical Engineering from Cornell University and an MBA from the School of Business, Villanova University.

Acknowledgments

This book reflects the effort, help, and support of many people without whom this book would not have been possible.

Special acknowledgments to our families for making this book come to life.

We would also like to acknowledge all of the individuals who made significant contributions toward the completion of this book, especially Ryan Ohlson, Michael Haller, and George Lemmon, whose detailed review and feedback was such a great help.

We extend our sincere thanks to all of you.

Preface

We wrote this book specifically for today's global financial and nonfinancial executives who are looking for an easy-to-use reference book on financial ratios and capital allocation to assist them in operational and strategic decision making. Our aim is to make financial ratios simple and intuitive for everyone to understand.

This book contains over one hundred financial ratios and other calculations commonly used in businesses around the world—including *return on investment* (ROI), *return on assets* (ROA), *return on equity* (ROE), *economic value added* (EVA), and *debt ratio* just to name a few.

We have also included a section on what financial and nonfinancial executives need to understand about capital allocation before entering the annual budget meeting or any other business meeting in which capital allocation is discussed. This section describes tools such as *net present value* (NPV), *internal rate of return* (IRR), the *payback method*, and *total cost of ownership*.

Given that a good understanding of financial ratios, valuation tools, and return on investment calculations are important components of any business system, we set out to create a simplified handbook with short descriptions, calculations, and examples for each of the ratios.

It is important to note that financial analysis is not always black and white. Two experienced finance people can sit down with identical financial information for a company, come up with different ratios, and both be right. Often, financial analysis is more of an art than a science. Accounting and business have their own language and, as with any language, sometimes the same words can have different meanings to different people. Always bear in mind that the particular meaning of a general ratio depends on context.

Consistency is key. Sometimes certain adjustments, such as non-recurring items, are made to specific line items, so as long as you are consistent in doing the same calculation year over year or when comparing companies against each other, your comparisons still have meaning. It may not matter if another accountant, colleague, or business manager gets a different answer; it is the internally consistent comparison and the underlying analysis that matter.

Microsoft Excel has built-in functions for some of the calculations in this book, such as IRR and NPV. The built-in functions may calculate ratios slightly different than the mathematical formulas do. Again, however, as long as you consistently use the same tool, any disparity between tools may not be analytically significant.

Some ratios are known by multiple names (e.g., the *acid test* is also known as the *quick ratio*). For completeness and easy reference, all ratios are duplicated under each name so no back-and-forth page turning is required.

In some of the examples we have also given our readers a sense of the normal ranges of values for specific ratios in various industries.

Remember, the tools described in this book are just that—tools. Whether one carpenter uses a hammer slightly differently than the next carpenter does not matter as long as the job gets done properly. Provided you use the tools in this book consistently and with good business judgment, they can help you make good business decisions.

Ratios Overview

The ratios in this book are tools. They are primarily tools for turning the data contained in financial statements into information used by managers and executives to better understand what is happening in a company. Like all tools, they can be used for things other than their original design, such as evaluating an acquisition, creating pro-forma statements related to potential courses of action, or figuring out which stock to buy.

Financial ratios can typically be grouped into one of the following ratio types:

- Market value ratios
- Liquidity ratios
- Performance ratios
- Cash flow ratios
- Profitability ratios
- Debt ratios

There are a small number of ratios that do not fit into any of these categories. However, we have included them as we have found them very useful ourselves and believe that they make for a more complete book.

Once a company has had several years of financial ratios, these can then be compared across these years to see if there is a positive or negative development. There are many ratios and all are great to use when a development is to be analyzed.

The following sections provide a short overview of each of the above ratio types along with a list of common examples, all of which will be defined and discussed in subsequent chapters.

Market value ratios

Market value ratios measure how cheap or expensive the company's stock is based on some measure of profit or value. Market value ratios can assist management or an investor in assessing the market's opinion of the company's value. Generally, the higher the market value ratio, the higher the company's stock price will be because the market thinks growth prospects are good and/ or they believe the company to be less risky as an investment.

Common market value ratios include the following:

- Dividend payout ratio
- Dividend yield
- Earnings per share (EPS)
- Enterprise value
- Price to book value ratio
- Price to earnings ratio (P/E ratio)

Liquidity ratios

Liquidity ratios measure the company's ability to pay off short-term debt obligations. Most obviously, they can be used to see if a company is in trouble and evaluate their ability to make loan payments or pay suppliers. Less obviously, they can be used to judge a company's ability to take on more debt, or spend more cash, to explore new means for growth through innovation or acquisition.

Common liquidity ratios include the following:

- Acid test
- Cash conversion cycle
- Cash ratio
- Current ratio
- Operating cash flow
- Quick ratio
- Working capital

Performance ratios

Performance ratios (also known as *activity ratios*) measure a company's ability to generate sales and derive profit from its resources. Performance ratios are used to measure the relative efficiency of a company based on the use of its assets, leverage, or other such balance sheet items.

Companies must often strike a balance between the inefficiencies of having too few or too many assets. For example, in the case of too little inventory, you may risk disruption to production and loss of sales. However, sitting on inventory that does not move is a very inefficient use of cash.

Common performance ratios include the following:

- Average collection period
- Fixed assets turnover
- Gross profit margin
- Inventory turnover
- Receivable turnover
- Total assets turnover

Cash flow ratios

Cash flow ratios measure how much cash is generated and the safety net that cash provides to the company to finance debt or grow the business. Cash flow ratios provide an additional way of looking at a company's financial health and performance. Many use the term "cash is king" because it is so vital to the health of an organization.

Common cash flow ratios include the following:

- Cash flow coverage
- Dividend payout ratio
- Free cash flow
- Operating cash flow

Profitability ratios

Profitability ratios can be thought of as the combination of many of the other more specific ratios to show a more complete picture of a company's ability to generate profits. The king of all ratios, return on equity (ROE), can be broken down by the DuPont formula in simple terms as ROE = Margin x Turn x Leverage. You can see how this takes into account other operating ratios. Many of the ratios in this section follow the same concept.

Common profitability ratios include the following:

- Current yield
- Profit margin
- Return on assets (ROA)
- Return on net assets (RONA)
- Return on equity (ROE)
- Return on investment (ROI)

Debt ratios

Debt ratios measure the company's overall debt load and the mix of equity and debt. Debt ratios give us a look at the company's leverage situation. Debt ratios can be good, bad, or indifferent, depending on a host of factors including who is asking. For example, a high total debt ratio may be good for stockholders not wanting to dilute their shares but bad for the creditors of the company.

Common debt ratios include the following:

- Asset to equity
- Asset turnover
- Cash flow to debt ratio
- Debt ratio
- Debt to equity
- Equity multiplier
- Interest coverage

Ratios Description

Each ratio or calculation in this book is presented on its dedicated page in the following standard format:

- Type of ratio (performance ratio, liquidity ratio, and so on)
- Formula for calculating the ratio
- Description of the ratio
- Example based on ABC Company or XYZ Company
- Synonyms (e.g., *quick ratio* is a synonym for *acid test*)

■ **Note**   For completeness and easy reference, each ratio synonym has its own dedicated page.

Most ratio calculations are based on data from the hypothetical ABC Company, whose financial data are listed in that company's income statement, balance sheet, cash flow statement, and additional company information given in Chapter 3.

Where the ABC Company data are not applicable to certain ratio calculations, we use data from the hypothetical XYZ Company.

Acid test (Quick ratio)

Type: Liquidity measure

Formula

$$\text{Acid test} = \frac{\text{Current assets} - \text{Inventory}}{\text{Current liabilities}}$$

Description

The *acid test ratio* shows whether a company has enough short-term assets to cover its immediate liabilities without selling inventory. The higher the acid test ratio, the safer a position the company is in.

Example

ABC Company has currents assets in the amount of $69,765, inventory in the amount of $24,875, and current liabilities in the amount of $28,500. This gives an acid test of 1.58. An acid test of 1.58 indicates that the company has sufficient current assets to cover its current liabilities more than one and a half times over without selling inventory.

$$\text{Acid test} = \frac{69,765 - 24,875}{28,500} = 1.58$$

The acid test is very similar to the current ratio except that it excludes inventory because inventory is often illiquid. The nature of the inventory and the industry in which the company operates will determine if the acid test or the current ratio is more applicable.

Note

The acid test is also known as the *quick ratio*.

Account receivable turnover (Receivable turnover)

Type: Performance measure

Formula

$$\text{Accounts receivable turnover} = \frac{\text{Sales}}{\text{Receivables}}$$

Description

The *accounts receivable turnover* measures the number of times receivables are converted into cash in a given period. This is different from the average collection period, which shows the number of days it takes to collect the receivables.

Ideally, credit sales should be used in the numerator and average receivables in the denominator. However, these are most often not easily available in the financial statements.

Example

ABC Company has sales in the amount of $210,000 and accounts receivable in the amount of $28,030. This gives an accounts receivable turnover ratio of 7.49. The higher the accounts receivable turnover ratio, the better the company is at converting receivables into cash. A decline in the turnover ratio could mean either a decline in sales or an indication that the customers are taking a longer time to pay for their purchases.

$$\text{Accounts receivable turnover} = \frac{210,000}{28,030} = 7.49$$

The company can improve the turnover ratio by many methods; the most popular is by offering a discount if the customers pay their outstanding balance earlier; for example, within 30 days of the sale.

Note

Accounts receivable turnover is also known as *receivable turnover*.

Additional funds needed (AFN)

Type: Other

Formula

$$\text{AFN} = \begin{array}{c} \text{Required} \\ \text{asset} \\ \text{increase} \end{array} - \begin{array}{c} \text{Spontaneous} \\ \text{liabilities} \\ \text{increase} \end{array} - \begin{array}{c} \text{Increase} \\ \text{in retained} \\ \text{earnings} \end{array}$$

Description

The *additional funds needed* (AFN) is an approximation tool to determine how much external funding a company would require in order to increase sales (if the company is operating at full capacity), given the amount of assets needed to generate those sales. AFN tells you how much outside cash a company needs to support linear growth. Because many of the factors used in AFN require estimation, you can see that AFN really only provides a ballpark figure.

Example

The AFN equation can be written as follows:

AFN = $(A_o/S_o)\ \Delta S - (L_o/S_o)\ \Delta S - M\ (S1) \times (1 - POR)$

- Required asset increase $(A_o/S_o)\ \Delta S$
- Spontaneous liabilities increase $(L_o/S_o)\ \Delta S$
- Increase in retained earnings $M\ (S1) \times (1 - POR)$

A_o	Total assets (Current year)	132,000
S_o	Sales (Current year)	210,000
ΔS	Change in sales (10% sales growth)	21,000
L_o	Spontaneous liabilities (accounts payables)	18,460
M	(Net) Profit margin	4.51%
S1	New sales (Original + Change in sales)	231,000
POR	Payout ratio (Dividend/Net income)	32%

Using the AFN formula, ABC Company would need an additional $4,223 to support a 10% increase in sales.

Altman's Z-Score

Type: Other

Formula

Z-Score = 1.2A + 1.4B + 3.3C + 0.6D + 1.0E

A = Working capital/Total assets

B = Retained earnings/Total assets

C = Earnings before interest & tax/Total assets

D = Market value of equity/Total liabilities

E = Sales/Total assets

Description

The *Altman's Z-Score* was developed to predict the probability that a company will go into bankruptcy within two years. The lower the Z-Score, the greater the probability the company will go into bankruptcy within the next two years. A score less than 1.8 indicates that the company is likely headed for bankruptcy, whereas a score above 3.0 indicates that the company has a low risk of bankruptcy.

Example

ABC Company has a Z-Score of 5.49. This means that there is a very low probability of the company going into bankruptcy within the next two years.

Z-Score = 1.2(1.29) + 1.4(0.36) + 3.3(0.42) + 0.6(0.77) + 1.0(1.59)
**   = 5.49**

A	B	C	D	F	G	H	I
1							
2	Factor	Nominator	Denominator	Result	Factor	Value	
3	A	41,265	32,000	1.29	1.20	1.55	
4	B	47,040	132,000	0.36	1.40	0.50	
5	C	13,525	32,000	0.42	3.30	1.39	
6	D	61,500	79,930	0.77	0.60	0.46	
7	E	210,000	132,000	1.59	1.00	1.59	
8	Z-Score					5.49	
9							

Asset to equity

Type: Debt measure

Formula

$$\text{Asset} - \text{to} - \text{equity} = \frac{\text{Total assets}}{\text{Shareholder equity}}$$

Description

The *asset-to-equity ratio* (also known as the *equity multiplier*) gives a sense of how much of the total assets of a company are really owned by shareholders as compared to those that are financed by debt. Some businesses thrive more on borrowing money (*leverage*) than other companies.

High assets-to-equity may be good for them. However, there is always some point for any company at which their assets are overleveraged. That can be dangerous to the shareholders and their investment in the company (e.g., Lehman Brothers was so overleveraged in 2007 that their asset-to-equity was 31! Calls on their debt in 2008 more than wiped out the company).

Example

ABC Company has total assets in the amount of $132,000 and shareholder equity in the amount of $52,070. This gives an asset-to-equity ratio of 2.54. Thus, the business has about $2.54 of assets for every dollar of shareholder equity.

$$\text{Asset} - \text{to} - \text{equity} = \frac{132,000}{52,070} = 2.54$$

Note

Debt financing typically offers a lower rate compared to equity. However, too much debt financing is rarely the optimal structure because debt has to be paid back even when the company is going through troubled times.

Asset turnover

Type: Performance measure

Formula

$$\text{Asset turnover} = \frac{\text{Sales}}{\text{Assets}}$$

Description

The *asset turnover ratio* measures the sales generated per dollar of assets and is an indication of how efficient the company is in utilizing assets to generate sales.

Asset-intensive companies such as mining, manufacturing, and so on will generally have lower asset turnover ratios compared to companies that have fewer assets, such as consulting and service companies.

Example

ABC Company has sales in the amount of $210,000 and total assets in the amount of $132,000. This gives an asset turnover ratio of 1.59.

$$\text{Asset turnover} = \frac{210,000}{132,000} = 1.59$$

This means that for every dollar invested in assets, the company generates $1.59 of sales. This number should be compared to the industry average for companies in the same industry.

Audit ratio

Type: Other

Formula

$$\text{Audit ratio} = \frac{\text{Annual audit fee}}{\text{Sales}}$$

Description

The *audit ratio* measures the cost of an audit in relation to the sales of the company. An increase in the audit ratio could indicate that additional audit procedures were required because of problems with the company's accounting records or control procedures. It could also indicate additional procedures were needed because of a change in legislation. When the Sarbanes-Oxley Act was written into law, it resulted in significant increases in audit fees as a result of additional testing and control procedures.

Example

ABC Company has sales in the amount of $210,000 and annual audit fees in the amount of $200. This results in an audit ratio of 0.095%.

$$\text{Audit ratio} = \frac{200}{210,000} = 0.095\%$$

Note

There is not always a direct correlation between the revenue and the annual audit fee, and it can vary significantly between various industries. However, as a company grows, so, typically, do the audit fees. Within the same company this number can be trended over time.

Average collection period

Type: Performance measure

Formula

$$\text{Average collection period} = \frac{\text{Days} \times \text{Accounts receivable}}{\text{Credit sales}}$$

Description

The *average collection period* indicates the amount of time (in days) it takes a company to convert its receivables into cash.

Example

ABC Company has accounts receivable in the amount of $28,030 and credit sales in the amount of $210,000. In this example, credit sales and total sales are identical. This gives an average collection period of 48.72 days, which means that it takes a little over one and a half months for the company to convert credit sales into cash.

$$\text{Average collection period} = \frac{365 \times 28,030}{210,000} = 48.72 \text{ days}$$

The company's credit terms will have a significant impact on the average collection period: the better the credit terms, the higher the average collection period. An increase in the average collection period could indicate an increased risk of the company's customers not being able to pay for their purchases. A possible result is that the company will have to hold greater levels of current assets as a reserve for potential losses or bad debt expense. Most large companies (nonretail) do not handle many cash sales. Therefore, when looking at financial statements, it can be assumed that total sales do not include any cash sales. However, in smaller companies and in retail businesses, cash sales can be a significant part of the total sales.

Note

The average collection period is also known as days sales outstanding.

Basic earning power (BEP)

Type: Profitability measure

Formula

$$\text{Basic earnings power} = \frac{\text{EBIT}}{\text{Total assets}}$$

Description

The *basic earning power* (BEP) shows the earning power of the company's assets before taxes and debt service. It is useful for comparing companies that otherwise could not be compared because of different tax situations and different degrees of financial leverage. This ratio is often used as a measure of the effectiveness of operations.

Example

ABC Company has earnings before interest and taxes (EBIT) in the amount of $13,525 and total assets in the amount of $132,500. This gives a basic earnings power ratio (BEP) of 0.10.

$$\text{Basic earnings power} = \frac{13,525}{132,500} = 0.10$$

This means that for every $100 invested in assets the company generates $10 of EBIT. This number can be compared to industry averages, or other companies, to gauge the operational effectiveness of generating profits.

Book value per share

Type: Market value measure

Formula

$$\text{Book value per share} = \frac{\text{Common equity}}{\text{Shares outstanding}}$$

Description

The *book value per share* measures common stockholders' equity determined on a per-share basis and is an indication of how the investors view the value of the company's assets. If the market value per share is higher than the book value per share, then the investor is willing to pay a premium over the book value to acquire the company's assets.

Example

ABC Company has common equity in the amount of $52,070 and a total of 10,000 shares outstanding. This gives a book value per share of $5.20 at December 31, 2013.

$$\text{Book value per share} = \frac{52,070}{10,000} = 5.20$$

ABC Company has a market value per share of $6.15. The reason could be that there are certain intangibles assets within the company such as customer list, distribution channels, or know-how, and so on, which the company cannot record as an asset under U.S. or international accounting standards. As a result of this, the investor is willing to pay a premium over book value to acquire the assets of the company.

$$
\begin{array}{lccc}
& \text{Assets} & = \text{Liabilities} & + \text{Equity} \\
\text{Market value} & 141,430 & = 79,930 & + 61,500
\end{array}
$$

With a share price of $6.15, the market value of the equity is $61,500, which means that the investor value the company's assets to $141.430, $9,430 over book value.

Breakeven point

Type: Cost accounting

Formula

$$\text{Breakeven point} = \frac{\text{Fixed cost}}{\text{Contribution margin ratio}}$$

Description

The *breakeven point*, often used in cost accounting, is the point at which the company breaks even on a given product and neither incurs a profit nor a loss. The breakeven point shows the minimum amount of sales required for the company to begin making a profit.

Example

XYZ Company is considering investing in a new production unit that costs $1,000,000 to support the increased demands in sales. The fixed cost for the new unit once installed is $200,000 annually. The company has calculated a contribution margin of 68%. This gives a breakeven point of $292,306, or 61,538 units.

$$\text{Breakeven point} = \frac{200,000}{0.68} = 292,306$$

This table shows that the company breaks even, meaning that it incurs neither a profit nor a loss, when it sells 61.538 units which amounts to sales of $292,306.

A	B	C	D	F	I
1					
2	Description	Units	Price	Total	
3	Sales	61,538	4.75	292,306	
4	Variable cost	(61,538)	1.50	(92,307)	
5	Fixed cost			(200,000)	
6	Break even			-	
7					

Capital asset pricing model (CAPM)

Type: Other

Formula

$$CAPM = Risk\ free\ rate + \big(Beta \times Market\ risk\ premium\big)$$

Description

The *capital asset pricing model* (CAPM) is a theoretical model used to determine the required rate of return for an investor when considering a particular stock to purchase. The stock's required rate of return is equal to the risk-free rate of return plus a risk premium reflecting only the risk remaining after diversification.

Investors most often use 10-year U.S. treasury bill or bond rate as a proxy for the risk-free rate. Beta is most often calculated by a third party and is available online. Market risk premium is the market rate of return less the risk-free rate. The market rate of return can be based on past returns. The economist Peter Bernstein calculated the average rate of return to be 9.6% over the past 200 years. This rate of return is often applied by investors when using the capital asset pricing model.

Example

An investor could use CAPM to determine the required rate of return to invest in ABC Company. If we assume that the rate of a 10-year U.S. treasury bill is 2%, the Beta for ABC Company is 0.9, and the market rate of return is 9.6%, we can calculate CAPM as follows:

$$CAPM = 0.02 + (0.9 \times \big(0.096 - 0.02\big) = 0.0884 = 8.84\%$$

By using CAPM, an investor can compare the required rate of return to an expected rate of return for the company over the investment horizon. If the investor does not think that the stock will yield a return of 8.84% over the investment period, he should not buy the stock.

Capital structure ratio

Type: Debt measure

Formula

$$\text{Capital structure ratio} = \frac{\text{Long} - \text{term debt}}{\text{Long} - \text{term debt} + \text{Shareholders equity}}$$

Description

The *capital structure ratio,* also known as the capitalization ratio, measures the debt component of a company's capital structure or how much of the company's financing is represented by long-term debt.

Example

ABC Company has long-term debt in the amount of $16,750 and equity in the amount of $52,070; this gives a capitalization ratio of 24.33%.

$$\text{Capital structure ratio} = \frac{16,750}{16,750 + 52,070} = 24.33\%$$

This capitalization ratio means that 24.33% of the company's operations and growth is financed by debt and 75.67% is financed by equity.

The amount of leverage that is right for the company varies based on the industry in which the company operates and the maturity of the company as well as other factors. What is optimal for one company might not be right for another. However, low debt and high equity levels in the capitalization ratio generally indicate lower risk for investors.

Note

Capitalization structure ratio is also known as capitalization ratio.

Capitalization ratio

Type: Debt measure

Formula

$$\text{Capitalization ratio} = \frac{\text{Long} - \text{term debt}}{\text{Long} - \text{term debt} + \text{Shareholders equity}}$$

Description

The *capitalization ratio*, also known as the capital structure ratio, measures the debt component of a company's capital structure or how much of the company's financing is represented by long-term debt.

Example

ABC Company has long-term debt in the amount of $16,750 and equity in the amount of $52,070; this gives a capitalization ratio of 24.33%.

$$\text{Capitalization ratio} = \frac{16,750}{16,750 + 52,070} = 24.33\%$$

This capitalization ratio means that 24.33% of the company's operations and growth is financed by debt and 75.67% is financed by equity.

The amount of leverage, that is, debt that is right for the company varies based on the industry in which the company operates and the maturity of the company as well as other factors. What is optimal for one company might not be right for another. However, low debt and high equity levels in the capitalization ratio generally indicate lower risk for the investors.

Note

Capitalization ratio is also known as capitalization structure ratio.

Cash conversion cycle (CCC)

Type: Liquidity measure

Formula

$$CCC = \begin{array}{c} \text{Days in} \\ \text{inventory} \end{array} + \begin{array}{c} \text{Days sales} \\ \text{outstanding} \end{array} - \begin{array}{c} \text{Days payable} \\ \text{outstanding} \end{array}$$

Description

The *cash conversion cycle* indicates the number of days that a company's cash is tied up in the production and sales process of its operations. The shorter the cycle, the more liquid the company's working capital is.

Example

ABC Company has currents days in inventory of 43.25 days, days sales outstanding of 48.72, and a days payable outstanding of 41.34 days. This gives a cash conversation cycle (CCC) of 50.63 days.

$$\text{Cash conversion cycle} = 43.25 + 48.72 - 41.34 = 50.63 \text{ days}$$

The higher the CCC, the longer it takes for the company to convert its inventory and credit sales into cash. An increase in the CCC could be an indication of one or all of the following:

- The company has a large amount of old or slow moving inventory that eventually will need to be written off.

- The customers are not paying as quickly as they have done in the past. This could lead to an increase in reserve for bad debt or possibly an expense for bad debt.

- Days payable outstanding has decreased as a result of the company paying its bills earlier than they have in the past.

Cash flow per share

Type: Profitability measure

Formula

$$\text{Cash flow per share} = \frac{\text{Operating cash flow} - \text{Preferred dividend}}{\text{Shares outstanding}}$$

Description

The *cash flow per share* ratio is very similar to earnings per share, but this ratio uses cash instead of earnings. Earnings can theoretically be manipulated from quarter to quarter more easily than cash can. Thus, tracking cash flow per share can show a better picture of what is going on with the company.

Some financial analysts place more emphasis on cash flow than earnings as a measure of the company's financial situation.

Example

ABC Company has operating cash flow in the amount of $8,145. There are no preferred shares in ABC Company; thus, there is no preferred dividend. Total number of shares outstanding amounts to 10,000. This gives a cash flow per share of $0.81 as of December 31, 2013.

$$\text{Cash flow per share} = \frac{8,145 - 0}{10,000} = 0.81$$

This number can be compared to industry averages or other companies in the same industry to compare operational effectiveness at generating cash.

Cash flow to debt ratio

Type: Debt measure

Formula

$$\text{Cash flow to debt ratio} = \frac{\text{Operating cash flow}}{\text{Total debt}}$$

Description

The *cash flow to debt ratio* indicates the company's ability to cover total debt with its annual cash flow from operations. A high cash flow to debt ratio puts the company in a strong position to cover its total debt.

Example

ABC Company has cash flow from operations in the amount of $8,145 and total debt (short term and long term) in the amount of $22,005. This gives a cash flow to debt ratio of 0.37.

$$\text{Cash flow to debt ratio} = \frac{8,145}{22,005} = 0.37$$

A cash flow to debt ratio of 0.37 indicates that it will take the company over three years (i.e., 3.7 times) to cover its total debt. This number can be compared to industry averages or other companies to compare debt loads.

Cash ratio

Type: Liquidity measure

Formula

$$\text{Cash ratio} = \frac{\text{Cash and cash equivalent}}{\text{Current liabilities}}$$

Description

The *cash ratio* measures the company's liquidity. It further refines both the current ratio and the quick ratio by measuring the amount of cash and cash equivalents there are in current assets to cover current liabilities.

Example

ABC Company has cash and cash equivalents in the amount of $16,450 and current liabilities in the amount of $28,500. This gives a cash ratio of 0.58.

$$\text{Cash ratio} = \frac{16,450}{28,500} = 0.58$$

This number can be compared to industry averages or other companies to compare liquidity.

This means that the company can pay off 58% of its current liabilities without generating additional cash.

Collection period

Type: Performance measure

Formula

$$\text{Collection period} = \frac{\text{Days} \times \text{Account receivable}}{\text{Credit sales}}$$

Description

The *collection period* indicates the amount of time (in days) that it takes a company to convert its receivables into cash.

Example

ABC Company has accounts receivable in the amount of $28,030 and credit sales in the amount of $210,000. In this example, credit sales and total sales are identical. This gives a collection period of 48.72 days, which means that it takes a little over one and a half months for the company to convert credit sales into cash.

$$\text{Collection period} = \frac{365 \times 28,030}{210,000} = 48.72 \text{ days}$$

The company's credit terms will have a significant impact on the average collection period: the better the credit terms, the higher the average collection period. An increase in the collection period could indicate increased risk of the company's customers not being able to pay for their purchases. A possible result is that the company will have to hold greater levels of current assets as a reserve for potential losses or bad debt expense. Most large companies (nonretail) do not handle many cash sales. Therefore, when looking at financial statements; it can be assumed that total sales do not include any cash sales. However, in smaller companies and in retail businesses, cash sales can be a significant part of the total sales.

Note

Collection period is also known as the average collection period or as days sales outstanding.

Compound annual growth rate (CAGR)

Type: Other

Formula

$$CAGR = \left(\left(\text{Ending value} / \text{Starting value} \right)^{1/(\text{number of periods})} \right) - 1$$

Description

The *compound annual growth rate* shows the average year over year growth rate for a given period. Compound annual growth rate over a given period is always a better indication than the use of a single year's change.

CAGR also eliminates spikes and drops (especially for companies that are very seasonal in nature) during the selected period and a good tool when comparing different companies growth rates.

Example

ABC Company has the following annual sales between 2011 and 2013, which means that there are two growth periods e.g., 2011 to 2012 is one growth period and 2012 to 2013 is another growth period:

> 2011 Sales: $175,182
>
> 2012 Sales: $203,700
>
> 2013 Sales: $210,000

$$CAGR = \left(\left(210,000 / 175,182 \right)^{(1/2)} \right) - 1 = 0.0949$$

The compound annual growth rate shows that the company's sales have increased 9.49% annually from 2011 to 2013.

To calculate the compound annual growth rate in Excel, the following formula can be typed into the formula bar:

$$=((210000/175182)^\wedge(1/2))-1)$$

Contribution margin

Type: Cost accounting

Formula

$$\text{Contribution margin} = \text{Sales} - \text{Variable cost}$$

Description

The *contribution margin* is the difference between sales and variable cost. The contribution margin can be calculated for the company as a whole or by product group or by individual units. The contribution margin shows the amount available to cover fixed cost and profit.

Example

XYZ Company is considering investing in a new production unit that costs $1,000,000 to support increased demands in sales. The fixed cost for the new unit is $200,000 annually. The new production unit can produce 240,000 units annually. The company expects to sell 135,000 units the first year at a sales price of 4.75 per unit, generating total sales of $641,250. The variable cost of each unit is $1.50 amounting to $202,500 in annual variable cost. This results in a contribution margin of $438,750 and a contribution margin ratio of 0.68%.

$$\text{Contribution margin} = 641,250 - 202,500 = 438,750$$

A	B	C	D	F	I
1					
2	Description	Units	Price	Total	
3	Sales	135,000	4.75	641,250	
4	Variable cost	135,000	1.50	202,500	
5	Contribution margin	135,000	3.25	438,750	
6	Contribution margin ratio			0.68	
7					

This means that the company has $438,750 to cover fixed cost and profit.

Contribution margin ratio

Type: Cost accounting

Formula

$$\text{Contribution margin ratio} = \frac{\text{Sales} - \text{Variable costs}}{\text{Sales}}$$

Description

The *contribution margin ratio* shows the percentage of sales available to cover fixed costs and profit. The contribution margin ratio can be calculated for the company as a whole or by product group or by individual units.

Example

XYZ Company is considering investing in a new production unit that costs $1,000,000 to support the increased demands in sales. The fixed cost for the new unit once installed is $200,000 annually. The new production unit can produce 240,000 units annually. The company expects to sell 135,000 units the first year at a sales price of 4.75 per unit, generating total sales of $641,250. The variable cost of each unit is $1.50 amounting to $202,500 in annual variable cost. This results in a contribution margin of $438,750 and a contribution margin ratio of 0.68%.

$$\text{Contribution margin ratio} = \frac{641,250 - 202,500}{641,250} = 0.68$$

A	B	C	D	F	I
1					
2	Description	Units	Price	Total	
3	Sales	135,000	4.75	641,250	
4	Variable cost	135,000	1.50	202,500	
5	Contribution margin	135,000	3.25	438,750	
6	Contribution margin ratio			0.68	
7					

This means that each dollar of sales generates $0.68 to cover fixed cost and profit.

Cost of capital (Weighted average cost of capital or WACC)

Type: Other

Formula

$$WACC = W_d \times R_d \times (1 - \text{Tax rate}) + W_{ps} \times R_{ps} + W_{cs} \times R_{cs}$$

Description

The *cost of capital,* also known as weighted average cost of capital or WACC, measures the company's average costs of financing. Companies have many sources of capital, mostly debt and equity.

WACC measures the weighted average cost of these two sources. This rate is most often used in capital allocation for evaluating future projects. In general, all projects that the company takes on should yield a return greater that the weighted average cost of capital.

Example

ABC Company has total debt in the amount of $79,930. The weight of the company's financing is 61% debt and 39% equity, the rate of which is financed at 7% and 13%, respectively. The company's effective tax rate is 22%. Tax rate used in the calculation should be the company's effective tax rate and not the statutory rate.

This gives a weighted average cost of capital in the amount of 8.40%. Projects that are not expected to return greater than 8.40% would generally be declined unless they show some other noneconomic benefit to the company.

$$WACC = 0.61 \times 0.07 \times (1 - 0.22) + 0 \times 0 + 0.39 \times 0.13 = 8.40\%$$

Note

W_d, W_{ps}, and W_{cs} are the weights (percentages) used for debt, preferred, and common shares, respectively. R_d, R_{ps}, and R_{cs} are the (interest) rates for debt, preferred, and common shares. Note that ABC Company has no preferred shares.

Current ratio

Type: Liquidity measure

Formula

$$\text{Current ratio} = \frac{\text{Current assets}}{\text{Current liabilities}}$$

Description

The *current ratio* indicates the extent to which current liabilities can be "covered" by current assets. Current assets include inventory, accounts receivable, cash, and securities. Current liabilities include accounts payable, short-term notes, current portion of long term debt, and accrued expenses.

Example

ABC Company has currents assets in the amount of $69,765 and current liabilities in the amount of $28,500. This gives a current ratio of 2.45.

$$\text{Current ratio} = \frac{69,765}{28,500} = 2.45$$

Thus, the company has almost two and a half times more current assets than current liabilities. This number is useful for comparison with industry trends but includes so many items from the financial statements that a deeper dive is often required to determine if a ratio is "good."

For example, a company using a just-in-time inventory system may have low inventory, making their current ratio lower but not necessarily indicating that there is a problem with meeting short-term obligations. Likewise, a company with bloated inventory may have a high current ratio and still have problems meeting short-term obligations.

Current yield (dividend yield)

Type: Profitability measure

Formula

$$\text{Current yield} = \frac{\text{Dividend per share}}{\text{Price per share}}$$

Description

The *current yield,* also known as dividend yield, is a measure of an investment's return. The higher the current yield, the higher the return on the investment.

Typically, only profitable companies pay out dividends; therefore, investors often view companies that have paid out significant dividends for an extended period of time as a less risky investment.

Example

ABC Company has paid out dividend per share in the amount of $0.30 and has a share price at the end of the year in the amount of $6.15 per share. This gives a current yield in the amount of 4.87%, which means that the investor has earned 4.87% return if he has paid $6.15 for each share purchased.

$$\text{Current yield} = \frac{0.30}{6.15} = 4.87\%$$

The term "yield" is often used in different situations to mean different things. Because of this, yields from different investments should not necessarily be compared as if they were all equal.

Note

The current yield is also known as dividend yield.

Days in inventory (Days inventory outstanding)

Type: Performance ratio

Formula

$$\text{Days in inventory} = \frac{\text{Inventory}}{\text{Cost of sales} / 365}$$

Description

The *days in inventory* ratio measures the average number of days the company holds its inventory before selling it to customers.

Example

ABC Company has inventory in the amount of $28,875 and cost of sales in the amount of $163,000. This gives days in inventory of 55.70 days.

$$\text{Days in inventory} = \frac{24,875}{163,000 / 365} = 55.70 \text{ days}$$

This means that ABC Company holds its inventory for an average of 55.70 days before their products are sold to customers. This number can be compared to the industry average, to other companies, or trended over time to see how a company is doing managing inventory.

The lower the number of days in inventory, the better the position of the company as cash is not tied up in inventory.

Note

Days in inventory is also known as days inventory outstanding and inventory conversion period.

Days inventory outstanding (Days in inventory)

Type: Performance measure

Formula

$$\text{Days inventory outstanding} = \frac{\text{Inventory}}{\text{Cost of sales} / 365}$$

Description

The *days inventory outstanding* ratio measures the average number of days that the company holds its inventory before selling it to customers.

Example

ABC Company has inventory in the amount of $28,875 and cost of sales in the amount of $163,000. This gives an inventory outstanding ratio of 55.70 days.

$$\text{Days inventory outstanding} = \frac{24,875}{163,000 / 365} = 55.70 \text{ days}$$

This means that ABC Company holds its inventory for an average of 55.70 days before their products are sold to customers. This number can be compared to the industry average, to other companies, or trended over time to see how a company is doing managing inventory.

The lower the number of days inventory outstanding the better the position of the company as cash is not tied up in inventory.

Note

Days inventory outstanding is also known as days in inventory and inventory conversion period.

Days payable (Payable period)

Type: Performance measure

Formula

$$\text{Days payable} = \frac{\text{Accounts payable}}{\text{Cost of sales} / 365}$$

Description

The *days payable* ratio, also known as payable period, measures a company's average number of days between receiving goods and paying its suppliers for them. The greater the payable period, the greater number of days it takes the company to pay its suppliers.

Example

ABC Company has accounts payable in the amount of $18,460 and credit purchase per day in the amount of $163,000. This gives days payable of 41.33 days.

$$\text{Days payable} = \frac{18,460}{163,000 / 365} = 41.33 \text{ days}$$

Days payable ratio of 41.33 means that the company pays its suppliers 41.33 days after receiving the products. The days payable period is a reflection of the credit terms that are extended to the company by its supplier. In general, a ratio much higher than the industry average could mean that the company has liquidity problems and that the company is not paying its suppliers in a timely manner.

A decline in the payable period could be an indication of change in credit terms or an indication that the company has issues with its cash management. This number can be compared to the industry average, to other companies, or trended over time to see how a company is doing with payables. This number can also be compared to known payment terms to see if the company is paying on time.

Days sales in cash

Type: Performance measure

Formula

$$\text{Days sales in cash} = \frac{\text{Cash and securities}}{\text{Annual sales} / 365}$$

Description

The *days sales in cash* ratio is a measure of management's control over cash balances. Generally, the more days sales in cash, the better the company's cash position, however, too many assets sitting in cash is not necessarily a good thing, either.

Example

ABC Company has cash and securities in the amount of $16,730 and annual sales in the amount of $210,000. This gives an average days sales in cash period of 29.08 days. This number can be compared to the industry average, to other companies, or trended over time to see how a company is managing cash.

$$\text{Days sales in cash} = \frac{16,730}{210,000 / 365} = 29.08 \text{ days}$$

Companies require a certain amount of cash for to make timely payments for its operations, i.e., vendor payments, payroll, etc. Companies with debt on its books may also have debt covenants that require them to have a certain amount on cash available.

Days sales outstanding (DSO)

Type: Performance measure

Formula

$$\text{Days sales outstanding} = \frac{\text{Days} \times \text{Account receivable}}{\text{Credit sales}}$$

Description

The *days sales outstanding,* also known as the average collection period, indicates the amount of time in days that it takes a company to convert its receivables into cash.

Example

ABC Company has accounts receivable in the amount of $28,030 and credit sales in the amount of $210,000. In this example, credit sales and total sales are identical. This gives days sales outstanding of 48.72 days, which means that it takes a little over one and a half months for the company to convert credit sales into cash.

$$\text{Days sales outstanding} = \frac{365 \times 28,030}{210,000} = 48.72 \text{ days}$$

The company's credit terms will have a significant impact on the average collection period: the better the credit terms, the higher the average collection period. An increase in days sales outstanding could indicate increased risk of the company's customers not being able to pay for their purchases. A possible result is that the company will have to reserve for potential losses or expense bad debt. Most large companies (nonretail) do not handle many cash sales. Therefore, when looking at financial statements, it can be assumed that total sales do not include any cash sales. However, in smaller companies and in retail businesses, cash sales can be a significant part of the total sales.

Note

Days sales outstanding is also known as average collection period or collection period.

Debt to assets

Type: Debt measure

Formula

$$\text{Debt to assets} = \frac{\text{Total debt}}{\text{Total assets}}$$

Description

The *debt to assets* ratio, also known as the debt ratio or debt to capital, shows the proportion of a company's total debt relative to its assets. This measure gives an idea as to the leverage of the company along with the potential risks the company faces in terms of its debt-load.

Example

ABC Company has total debt (total liabilities) in the amount of $79,930 and total assets in the amount of $132,000. This gives a debt to asset ratio of 0.61. This means that 61% of the company's assets are financed by the creditors and debt, and therefore 39% is financed by the owners (equity). A higher percentage indicates more leverage and more risk.

$$\text{Debt to assets} = \frac{79,930}{132,000} = 0.61$$

The amount of leverage, that is, debt that is right for the company varies based on the industry in which the company operates and the maturity of the company as well as other factors. What is optimal for one company might not be right for another. However, lower debt and higher equity levels generally indicate lower risk for the investors. The debt to asset ratio can be compared to the industry average, to other companies, or trended over time to see how a company is doing managing its debt.

Note

Debt to assets is also known as debt ratio or debt to capital.

Debt to capital ratio

Type: Debt measure

Formula

$$\text{Debt to capital} = \frac{\text{Total liabilities}}{\text{Total liabilities} + \text{book value of equity}}$$

Description

The *debt to capital ratio,* also known as debt ratio or debt to asset ratio, shows the proportion of a company's total debt relative to its assets. This measure gives an idea as to the leverage of the company along with the potential risks the company faces in terms of its debt-load.

Example

ABC Company has total debt (total liabilities) in the amount of $79,930 and total assets in the amount of $132,000. This gives a debt to capital ratio of 0.61. This means that 61% of the company's assets are financed by the creditors and debt, and therefore 39% is financed by the owners (equity). A higher percentage indicates more leverage and more risk.

$$\text{Debt to capital} = \frac{79,930}{79,930 + 52,070} = 0.61$$

The amount of leverage, that is, debt that is right for the company varies based on the industry in which the company operates and the maturity of the company as well as other factors. What is optimal for one company might not be right for another. However, lower debt and higher equity levels generally indicate lower risk for the investors. The debt to capital ratio can be compared to the industry average, to other companies, or trended over time to see how a company is doing managing its debt.

Note

Debt to capital is also known as debt ratio or debt to asset.

Debt ratio

Type: Debt measure

Formula

$$\text{Debt ratio} = \frac{\text{Total liabilities}}{\text{Total assets}}$$

Description

The *debt ratio,* also known as debt to asset ratio or debt to capital ratio, shows the proportion of a company's total debt relative to its assets. This measure gives an idea as to the leverage of the company along with the potential risks the company faces in terms of its debt-load.

Example

ABC Company has total liabilities in the amount of $79,930 and total assets in the amount of $132,000. This gives a debt ratio of 0.61. This means that 61% of the company's assets are financed by the creditors and debt, and therefore 39% is financed by the owners (equity). A higher percentage indicates more leverage and more risk.

$$\text{Debt ratio} = \frac{79,930}{132,000} = 0.61$$

The amount of leverage, that is, debt that is right for the company varies based on the industry in which the company operates and the maturity of the company as well as other factors. What is optimal for one company might not be right for another. However, lower debt and higher equity levels generally indicate lower risk for the investors. The debt ratio can be compared to the industry average, to other companies, or trended over time to see how a company is doing managing its debt.

Note

Debt ratio is also known as debt to assets or debt to capital ratio.

Debt to equity

Type: Debt measure

Formula

$$\text{Debt to equity} = \frac{\text{Total liabilities}}{\text{Total equity}}$$

Description

The *debt to equity* measures how much of the company is financed by its debt holders compared with its owners and is another measure of financial health. A company with a large amount of debt will have a very high debt to equity ratio, whereas one with little debt will have a low debt to equity ratio. Companies with lower debt to equity ratios are generally less risky than those with higher debt to equity ratios.

Example

ABC Company has total liabilities in the amount of $51,430 and equity in the amount of $52,070. This gives a debt to equity ratio of 0.98.

$$\text{Debt to equity} = \frac{51,430}{52,070} = 0.98$$

A debt to equity ratio of 0.98 is not uncommon. However, there is no specific optimal capital structure for a company. What is optimal for one company might not be right for another. There needs to be a balance between debt and equity financing. Debt financing typically offers the lowest rate. However, too much debt financing is rarely the optimal structure, as debt has to be paid back even when the company is going through troubled times.

Dividend payout ratio

Type: Market value measure

Formula

$$\text{Dividend payout ratio} = \frac{\text{Annual dividend per share}}{\text{Earnings per share}}$$

Description

The *dividend payout ratio* shows the percentage of earnings paid to shareholders in dividends and how well earnings support the dividend payments. More mature companies tend to have a higher payout ratio compared to growth companies. This is because growth companies can provide a higher return on investment by using the cash (dividend) to invest in the growth of the company.

Example

ABC Company has a dividend per share in the amount of $0.30 and earnings per share in the amount of $0.95. This gives a dividend payout ratio of 31.57%, which means that ABC Company paid 31.57% of its net income to its shareholders in form of dividend.

$$\text{Dividend payout ratio} = \frac{0.30}{0.95} = 31.57\%$$

Dividend payout ratio can also be calculated as dividends divided by net income. In this example, using the data from ABC Company, it would have been 3,000 / 9,475 = 31.57%.

This number can be compared to the industry average or to other companies to evaluate potential investments.

Dividend per share

Type: Market value measure

Formula

$$\text{Dividend per share} = \frac{\text{Dividend}}{\text{Shares outstanding}}$$

Description

The *dividend per share* ratio measures the profit distribution paid out on a per share basis to the company's shareholders. Most companies have a dividend payout policy; however, not all companies pay out an annual dividend. Growth companies would typically not pay out any dividend early on, whereas more mature companies typically pay out dividends. This is because growth companies can provide a higher return on investment, by using the cash (dividend) to invest in the growth of the company.

Example

ABC Company has paid out dividend in the amount of $3,000 based on a total number of outstanding shares of 10.000. This gives a dividend per share of 0.30 dollars.

$$\text{Dividend per share} = \frac{3,000}{10,000} = 0.30$$

A company with a year over year growth in the dividend per share is a positive sign that the company believes that the growth can be sustained. The growth in the dividend payout will also reflect positively on the company's share price.

This number can be compared to the industry average or to other companies to evaluate potential investments.

Dividend yield (Current yield)

Type: Profitability measure

Formula

$$\text{Dividend yield} = \frac{\text{Dividend per share}}{\text{Price per share}}$$

Description

The *dividend yield,* also known as current yield, is a measure of an investment's return. The higher the dividend yield, the higher the return on the investment.

Typically, only profitable companies pay out dividends; therefore, investors often view companies that have paid out significant dividends for an extended period of time as a less risky investment.

Example

ABC Company has paid out dividend per share in the amount of $0.30 and has a share price at the end of the year in the amount of $6.15 per share. This gives a dividend yield in the amount of 4.87%, which means that the investor has earned 4.87% return if he has paid $6.15 for each share purchased.

$$\text{Dividend yield} = \frac{0.30}{6.15} = 4.87\%$$

The term yield is often used in different situations to mean different things. Because of this, yields from different investments should not necessarily be compared as if they were all equal.

Note

The dividend yield is also known as current yield.

DuPont ratio

Type: Profitability measure

Formula

$$ROE = \text{Profit margin} \times \text{Total asset turnover} \times \text{Equity multiplier}$$

$$ROE = \frac{\text{Net income}}{\text{Sales}} \times \frac{\text{Sales}}{\text{Total assets}} \times \frac{\text{Total assets}}{\text{Equity}}$$

$$ROE = \frac{\text{Net income}}{\text{Equity}}$$

Description

The *DuPont ratio* is an expression that breaks return on equity (ROE) into its three components to give a total picture of how the company is performing. In the DuPont formula, ROE is defined as profit margin multiplied by total asset turnover and the equity multiplier. When someone says "DuPont ratio" and you instantly think "margin-turn-leverage," you are doing pretty well. What is important are the components, not necessarily the final number. Two companies might have the exact same ROE, but their components could be very different, showing you different business strategies.

Example

$$ROE = 0.05 \times 1.59 \times 2.54 = 0.18$$

$$ROE = \frac{9,475}{210,000} \times \frac{210,000}{132,000} \times \frac{132,000}{52,070} = 0.18$$

$$ROE = \frac{9.475}{52,070} = 0.18$$

Note

The DuPont Corporation started using this formula in the 1920s, hence the name.

Earnings before interest and taxes (EBIT)

Type: Performance measure

Formula

$$EBIT = Sales - Operating\ expenses$$

Description

The *earnings before interest and taxes*, also known as profit before interest & taxes (PBIT), is equivalent to net income with interest and taxes added back. EBIT is an indicator of the company's financial performance and provide investors useful information for evaluating different companies without regard to interest expenses or tax rates. By dropping interest and taxes from earnings, you normalize for companies with different capital structure and tax rates resulting in "apples-to-apples" comparisons.

Example

ABC Company has sales in the amount of $210,000 and operating expenses in the amount of $196,475. This amounts to $13,525 of EBIT.

$$EBIT = 2\,10,000 - 196,475 = 13,525$$

This number can be compared to other companies to evaluate potential investments, or to evaluate general profitability. EBIT is often included as a component of other ratio calculations such as basic earnings power, NOPAT, and times interest earned.

Note

EBIT, although not a measure defined by accounting principles generally accepted in the United States, is a financial performance indicator often used by management.

Earnings before interest, taxes, depreciation and amortization

Type: Performance measure

Formula

$$EBITDA = EBIT + Depreciation + Amortization$$

Description

The *earnings before interest, taxes, depreciation, and amortization* (EBITDA) although not a measure defined by accounting principles generally accepted in the United States, is a financial performance indicator often used by management. EBITDA is like EBIT but further eliminates depreciation and amortization (noncash expenses). Thus, EBITDA makes for "apples-to-apples" comparisons for companies by eliminating capital structure, taxes, and depreciation and amortization schedule differences.

Example

ABC Company has EBIT in the amount of $13,525 and depreciation and amortization in the amount of $100 and $375, respectively. This gives an EBITDA of $14,000.

$$EBITDA = 13,525 + 100 + 375 = 14,000$$

This number can be compared to other companies to evaluate potential investments, or to evaluate general profitability. EBITDA is often used in other ratio calculations and can often be found in the footnotes to the financial statements.

Some companies also use an adjusted EBITDA, a supplemental measure in evaluating the performance of the company's business. Adjusted EBITDA eliminates nonrecurring items from the calculation such as impairment of assets, write-off of goodwill, and so on. EBITDA and adjusted EBITDA often provide investors with better information in respect to a company's operations and financial condition.

EBIT

Type: Performance measure

Formula

$$EBIT = Sales - Operating\ expenses$$

Description

EBIT means *earnings before interest and taxes*, also known as profit before interest & taxes (PBIT) and is equivalent to net income with interest and taxes added back. EBIT is an indicator of the company's financial performance and provide investors useful information for evaluating different companies without regard to interest expenses or tax rates. By dropping interest and taxes from earnings, you normalize for companies with different capital structure and tax rates resulting in "apples-to-apples" comparisons.

Example

ABC Company has sales in the amount of $210,000 and operating expenses in the amount of $196,475. This amounts to $13,525 of EBIT.

$$EBIT = 210,000 - 196,475 = 13,525$$

This number can be compared to other companies to evaluate potential investments, or to evaluate general profitability. EBIT is often included as a component of other ratio calculations such as basic earnings power, NOPAT, and times interest earned.

Note

EBIT, although not a measure defined by accounting principles generally accepted in the United States, is a financial performance indicator often used by management.

EBITDA

Type: Performance measure

Formula

$$EBITDA = EBIT + Depreciation + Amortization$$

Description

EBITDA means *earnings before interest, taxes, depreciation, and amortization.* Although not a measure defined by accounting principles generally accepted in the United States, is a financial performance indicator often used by management. EBITDA is like EBIT but further eliminates depreciation and amortization (noncash expenses). Thus, EBITDA makes for "apples-to-apples" comparisons for companies by eliminating capital structure, taxes, and depreciation and amortization schedule differences.

Example

ABC Company has EBIT in the amount of $13,525 and depreciation and amortization in the amount of $100 and $375, respectively. This gives an EBITDA of $14,000.

$$EBITDA = 13,525 + 100 + 375 = 14,000$$

This number can be compared to other companies to evaluate potential investments, or to evaluate general profitability. EBITDA is often used in other ratio calculations and can often be found in the footnotes to the financial statements.

Some companies also use an adjusted EBITDA, a supplemental measure in evaluating the performance of the company's business. Adjusted EBITDA eliminates nonrecurring items from the calculation such as impairment of assets, write-off of goodwill, and so on. EBITDA and adjusted EBITDA often provide investors with better information in respect to a company's operations and financial condition.

EBITDA to interest coverage

Type: Debt measure

Formula

$$\text{EBITDA to interest coverage} = \frac{\text{EBITDA}}{\text{Interest payments}}$$

Description

The *EBITDA to interest coverage* ratio this ratio gives a measure of how much leverage a company can sustain. By eliminating the noncash depreciation and amortization expenses, it gives a truer sense of how much cash the company will have to cover interest payments. The lower the ratio, the higher the likelihood that the company will not be able to service their debts, that is, pay interest expenses on its debt.

Example

ABC Company has EBITDA in the amount of $14,000 and interest expenses in the amount of $1,190. This gives an EBITDA to interest coverage ratio in the amount of 11.76, which means that the company has earnings more than 11 times its interest expense.

$$\text{EBITDA to interest coverage} = \frac{14,000}{1,190} = 11.76$$

An EBITDA to interest coverage ratio of 11.76 provides sufficient coverage and indicates that the company will be able to service its debt. This number can be compared to other companies to evaluate potential investments or company performance relative to peer firms.

Earnings per share (EPS)

Type: Market value measure

Formula

$$EPS = \frac{Net\ income - Dividend\ on\ preferred\ shares}{Average\ outstanding\ shares}$$

Description

The *earnings per share* ratio shows the portion of a company's profit allocated to each outstanding share of common stock. Earnings per share serve as an indicator of a company's profitability.

Example

In 2013, ABC Company had net income in the amount of $9,475 and total number of outstanding shares of 10,000. This gives earnings per share of $0.95, which means that the company generates net income of $0.95 for each outstanding share.

$$EPS = \frac{9,475 - 0}{10,000} = 0.95$$

Generally, the higher the earnings per share the better a company is doing for the shareholders. An increase in EPS year over year is typically a sign of a growth or a mature company. Some companies buy back shares to improve earnings per share without necessarily increasing net income. It is therefore important to not only look at EPS in isolation but to compare EPS to the total number of shares outstanding.

Economic value added (EVA)

Type: Performance measure

Formula

$$EVA = \text{Total net operating capital} \times (ROIC - WACC)$$

Description

The *economic value added* measures a company's true profitability. That is, its ability to generate returns in excess of the return required by investors. If EVA is positive the company has created value for its shareholders. If EVA is negative, shareholder value has been destroyed.

Example

ABC Company has total net operating capital in the amount of $99,605, return on invested capital of 12.44% and WACC of 8.40%. This gives economic value added in the amount of $4,024.

$$EVA = 99,605 \times (0.1244 - 0.0840) = 4,024$$

This positive EVA can be interpreted as healthy, but it can also be compared to the EVA of other companies in a similar industry, or compared to the EVA of other potential investments.

Note

ROIC and WACC are explained elsewhere in this book.

Effective tax rate

Type: Profitability measure

Formula

$$\text{Effective tax rate} = \frac{\text{Tax expense}}{\text{Earnings before tax}}$$

Description

The *effective tax rate* explains the various rates at which a company's income is taxed as a result of different tax jurisdictions both domestically and internationally. Companies also employ strategies to minimize tax. To compute the effective (or average for the year) tax rate, total tax expense is divided by earnings before tax.

Example

ABC Company has total tax expenses for the year in the amount of $2,970 and earnings before tax in the amount of $12,445. This gives an effective tax rate of 23.86%.

$$\text{Effective tax rate} = \frac{2,970}{12,445} = 23.86\%$$

This number can be compared to other companies' effective tax rates to evaluate the tax strategies of the company. If, for example, you were Coke and you saw that Pepsi had a lower effective tax rate, you would want to do a deeper dive and find out why.

Note

Companies with significant lower than average tax rate compared to other companies in its industry might be very aggressive on their tax strategies. This could pose a risk of tax exposure in the form of a tax audit with reversal of the chosen tax treatment and could also result in tax penalties and other fees.

Enterprise value (EV)

Type: Market value measure

Formula

$$EV = \underset{\text{cap}}{\text{Market}} + \text{Debt} + \underset{\text{interest}}{\text{Minority}} + \underset{\text{shares}}{\text{Preferred}} - \underset{\substack{\text{cash} \\ \text{equivalents}}}{\text{Cash and}}$$

Description

The *enterprise value* is a measure of a company's value as a functioning entity, often used as an alternative to straightforward market capitalization. If you were to purchase (buy out) a firm, you would start with its enterprise value and work from there to determine your offer. Thus, you can see why cash is subtracted because you would get that cash in the deal to offset what you are buying, debt and equity.

Example

ABC Company has a market cap of $61,500, debt in the amount of $22,005, and cash and cash equivalents amounting to $16,450. The company does not have any minority interest or any preferred shares. This gives an enterprise value of $67,055.

$$EV = 61,500 + 22,005 + 0 + 0 - 16,450 = 67,055$$

Note

Calculating the enterprise value for public companies are relatively easy as the market cap—that is, the number of shares times the company's share price—is publicly available. Calculating the enterprise value for private companies are for the same reason not that easy as there is no public market for the company's stock. A common approach to valuing equity of a private company is to compare the entity to similar companies, that is, industry, debt structure, results, and growth opportunities, which are public traded.

Equity multiplier

Type: Debt measure

Formula

$$\text{Equity multiplier} = \frac{\text{Total asset}}{\text{Shareholder equity}}$$

Description

The *equity multiplier,* also known as assets to equity ratio, gives a sense of how much of the total assets of a company are really owned by shareholders as compared to those that are financed by debt. Some businesses thrive more on borrowing money (leverage) than other companies. High assets to equity may be good for them. However, there is always some point for any company for which their assets are overleveraged. That can be dangerous to the shareholders and their equity (e.g., Lehman Brothers was so overleveraged in 2007 that their assets to equity was 31! Calls on their debt in 2008 more than wiped out the shareholders).

Example

ABC Company has total assets in the amount of $132,000 and shareholder equity in the amount of $52,070. This gives an equity multiplier of 2.54. Thus, the business has $2.54 of assets for every dollar of shareholder equity.

$$\text{Equity multiplier} = \frac{132,000}{52,070} = 2.54$$

Note

Debt financing typically offers a lower rate compared to equity. However, too much debt financing is rarely the optimal structure as debt has to be paid back even when the company is going through troubled times.

Exercise value

Type: Other

Formula

$$\text{Exercise value} = \text{Current price of stock} - \text{Strike price}$$

Description

The *exercise value* is the value of an option if it is exercised today. For a call option, this is the difference between the current stock price and the strike price. The strike price, also known as the exercise price, is the current market value price.

Example

As part of his compensation, an ABC employee received 1,000 stock options with a strike price of $5.68. The shares are fully vested and can be exercised at any given time.

$$\text{Exercise value} = 6.15 - 5.68 = 0.47$$

Assuming that the employee wants to sell these shares on December 31 when the price per share is $6.15, the employee would receive cash in the amount of $0.47 per share amounting to $470.

$$\text{Cash payout} = \text{Number of shares} \times \text{Exercise value}$$

$$\text{Cash payout} = 1{,}000 \times 0.47 = \$470.00$$

Fixed assets turnover

Type: Performance measure

Formula

$$\text{Fixed assets turnover} = \frac{\text{Sales}}{\text{Total fixed assets}}$$

Description

The *fixed assets turnover* measures how effectively the company uses its assets to generate sales. The higher the ratio, the better the company is at generating sales from its assets.

The fixed assets typically include property, plant, and equipment. Other assets such as goodwill, deferred taxes, and other nonproperty, plant, and equipment items are typically excluded to provide a more meaningful and comparative ratio. In most cases, these assets are not directly involved in generating sales and are therefore excluded.

Example

ABC Company has sales in the amount of $210,000 and total fixed assets in the amount of $32,620, which gives a fixed asset turnover ratio of 6.44. This means that for each dollar invested in fixed assets the company is generating $6.44 of sales.

$$\text{Fixed assets turnover} = \frac{210,000}{32,620} = 6.44$$

Fixed asset turnover varies significantly from industry to industry. For example, a manufacturing company will have a much lower fixed asset turnover compared to a service company with little to no assets. It is therefore important to compare the ratio with comparable companies. A sudden decline in the fixed asset turnover ratio could be an indication that that the company has recently invested significantly in fixed assets. A decline could also indicate that the company has sold fixed assets or fully depreciated assets without acquiring new assets.

Free cash flow (FCF)

Type: Cash flow measure

Formula

$$\text{Free cash flow} = \text{NOPAT} - \text{Net investment in operating capital}$$

Description

The *free cash flow* shows the cash flow available for distribution after the company has made all investments in fixed assets and working capital necessary to sustain ongoing operations.

Net investment in operating capital is calculated by subtracting the previous year's total net operating capital from the current year's total net operating capital.

Example

ABC Company has NOPAT in the amount of $10,298 and capital expenditure in the amount of $5,165. This gives a free cash flow of $5,133 as of December 31, 2013.

$$\text{Free cash flow} = 10,298 - 5,165 = 5,133$$

This means that ABC Company could distribute $5,133 to its shareholders while sustaining their ongoing operations.

Note

NOPAT is calculated elsewhere in the book.

Gearing

Type: Debt management measure

Formula

$$\text{Gearing} = \frac{\text{Total liabilities}}{\text{Total equity}}$$

Description

One of the most common debt ratios is *gearing*. This ratio measures how much of the company is financed by its debt holders compared with its owners and it is another measure of financial health. A company with a large amount of debt will have a very gearing ratio, whereas one with little debt will have a low gearing ratio. Companies with lower gearing ratios are generally less risky than those with higher gearing ratios.

Example

ABC Company has total liabilities in the amount of $51,430 and equity in the amount of $52,070 this give a debt to equity ratio of 0.98.

$$\text{Gearing} = \frac{51,430}{52,070} = 0.98$$

A Gearing ratio of 0.98 is not uncommon. However, there is no specific optimal capital structure for a company. There needs to be a balance between debt (including short- and long-term debt) and equity financing. Debt financing typically offers the lowest rate because of its tax deductibility. However, too much debt financing is rarely the optimal structure as debt has to be paid back even when the company is going through troubled times.

Gordon constant growth model

Type: Market value measure

Formula

$$\text{Stock value} = \frac{\text{Expected dividend per share one year from now}}{\text{Required rate of return} - \text{Growth rate in dividends}}$$

Description

The *Gordon constant growth model* shows the intrinsic value of a stock based on future dividends at a constant growth rate. The model is mainly used to determine the intrinsic value of mature companies because of the constant growth rate component.

Example

Let's assume that ABC Company expects the growth rate in dividends to be 5% in perpetuity. The dividend per share in 2013 was $0.30. This means that the expected dividend per share for 2014 will be $0.315.

$$\text{Stock value} = \frac{0.315}{0.08 - 0.05} = 10.50$$

If we further assume that the investors required rate of return is 8%, then the intrinsic value of the stock would be $10.50. Compared to the current stock price of $6.15, this would make it a good stock in which to invest.

Gross profit margin

Type: Performance measure

Formula

$$\text{Gross profit margin} = \frac{\text{Sales} - \text{Cost of goods sold}}{\text{Sales}}$$

Description

The *gross profit margin* measures how much gross profit is generated for each dollar of sales. The gross profit has to cover the company's operating expenses, depreciation and amortization, finance cost, and taxes.

Gross profit margin will vary significantly between companies in different industries. For example, companies with significant fixed assets will typically have a higher gross profit margin than companies with low fixed assets such as service companies.

Example

ABC Company has sales in the amount of $210,000 and cost of sales in the amount of $163,000, which gives a gross profit margin of 22.38%. A gross profit margin of 22.38% means that for each $100 of sales generated by the company, $22.38 is gross profit to cover the company's operating costs.

$$\text{Gross profit margin} = \frac{210,000 - 163,000}{210,000} = 22.38\%$$

A change in the company's gross profit margin could be a result of price pressure from competitors, meaning that the company maintains the current cost structure while lowering sales prices. It could also be a result of higher cost of sales. This could be true if goods are imported, which typically adds another layer of expenses to the cost of sales, that is, fluctuations in foreign currents. Often, it can also be explained with a shift in product mix. It is therefore important to look at the gross profit margin on each product or product line.

Horizon value (Terminal value)

Type: Other

Formula

$$\text{Horizon value} = \frac{FCF \times (1 + \text{growth rate})}{WACC - \text{growth rate}}$$

Description

The *horizon value,* also known as the terminal value, shows the value of future operations beyond the end of the forecast period. It is calculated as the present value of all future cash flows after the forecast period.

That is the period when the company expects a constant growth rate in perpetuity. Horizon value is often used in valuation models for the period beyond which you don't have specific financial data but expect the company to grow at some constant rate.

Example

ABC Company has free cash flow in the amount of $5,360, WACC in the amount of 8.4%, and an assumed constant growth rate of 3%. This gives a horizon value in the amount of $102,237.

$$\text{Horizon value} = \frac{5,360 \times (1 + 0.03)}{8.4\% - 3.0\%} = 102,237$$

Note

The Horizon value is also known as the terminal value.

Interest coverage

Type: Debt measure

Formula

$$\text{Interest coverage} = \frac{\text{EBIT}}{\text{Interest expense}}$$

Description

The *interest coverage,* also known as times interest earned (TIE), indicates the company's ability to pay interest on its outstanding debt and to what extent operating income can decline before the company is unable to meet its annual interest expenses.

The lower the ratio, the higher the likelihood that the company will not be able to service its debt (pay interest expenses on its debt). If the interest coverage ratio gets below 1, the company is not generating enough earnings to service its debt.

Example

ABC Company has earnings before interest and taxes (EBIT) in the amount of $13,525 and interest expenses in the amount of $1,190. This gives an interest coverage ratio in the amount of 11.37, which means that the company has earnings more than 11 times its interest expense.

$$\text{Interest coverage} = \frac{13,525}{1,190} = 11.37$$

An interest coverage ratio of 11.37 provides sufficient coverage that the company will be able to service its debt.

Note

Interest coverage is also known as time interest earned ratio.

Inventory conversion period

Type: Performance measure

Formula

$$\text{Inventory conversion period} = \frac{\text{Inventory}}{\text{Cost of sales} / 365}$$

Description

The *inventory conversion period* measures the average number of days the company holds its inventory before selling it to customers.

Example

ABC Company has inventory in the amount of $28,875 and cost of sales in the amount of $163,000. This gives an inventory conversion period of 55.70 days.

$$\text{Inventory conversion period} = \frac{24,875}{163,000 / 365} = 55.70 \text{ days}$$

This means that ABC Company holds its inventory for an average of 55.70 days before their products are sold to customers. This number can be compared to the industry average, to other companies, or trended over time to see how a company is doing managing inventory.

The lower the inventory conversation period, the better position for the company from a cash management perspective as inventory is converted faster.

Note

Inventory conversion period is also known as days inventory outstanding and days in inventory.

Inventory turnover

Type: Performance measure

Formula

$$\text{Inventory turnover} = \frac{\text{Sales}}{\text{Inventory}}$$

Description

The *inventory turnover* shows how many times a company's inventory is sold and replaced over a given period. Inventory turnover for a period can also be calculated as cost of goods sold over ending inventory for that period.

Example

ABC Company has sales in the amount of $210,000 and inventory in the amount of $24,875; this gives an inventory turnover ratio of 8.44.

$$\text{Inventory turnover} = \frac{210,000}{24,875} = 8.44$$

COGS can also be used here to give a more accurate number but most industry publications use sales (which is inflated by the difference between retail price and COGS).

Using the inventory at a specific time may make the ratio less accurate. For the sake of comparison, it is better to use an average inventory, especially if the business is seasonal in nature.

Leverage

Type: Debt measure

Formula

$$\text{Leverage} = \frac{\text{Total debt}}{\text{Total equity}}$$

Description

The most well-known financial *leverage* ratio is the debt to equity ratio. This leverage ratio measures how much of the company is financed by its debt holders compared with its owners and it is another measure of financial health. A company with a large amount of debt will have a very high debt to equity ratio, whereas one with little debt will have a low debt to equity ratio. Companies with lower leverage are generally less risky than those with higher debt to equity ratios.

Example

ABC Company has total liabilities in the amount of $51,430 and equity in the amount of $52,070; this gives a debt to equity ratio of 0.98.

$$\text{Leverage} = \frac{51,430}{52,070} = 0.98$$

A debt to equity ratio of 0.98 is not uncommon. However, there is no specific optimal capital structure for a company. There needs to be a balance between debt and equity financing. Debt financing typically offers the lowest rate. However, too much debt financing it is rarely the optimal structure as debt has to be paid back even when the company is going through troubled times.

Market capitalization (Market cap)

Type: Market value measure

Formula

$$\text{Market Cap} = \text{Stock price} \times \text{Number of shares outstanding}$$

Description

The *market capitalization* (market cap), also known as market value of equity, is the total market value of all of a company's outstanding shares. Market cap is calculated by multiplying the company's shares outstanding by the current share price. Investors often use market cap to determine a company's size, as opposed to sales or total asset figures.

Example

ABC Company has a stock price of $6.15 per share at December 31, 2013 and 10,000 of shares outstanding. This gives a market cap of $61,500.

$$\text{Market Cap} = 6.15 \times 10,000 = 61,500$$

Note

Market capitalization is also known as market value of equity.

Market to book ratio

Type: Market value measure

Formula

$$\text{Market to book} = \frac{\text{Market price per share}}{\text{Book value per share}}$$

Description

The *market to book ratio,* also known as price to book ratio, measures the relative value of a company compared to its share price. The ratio can also be calculated as total market value over total book value as the "per share" part of the equation cancels out.

Market to book ratio is a great tool to quickly determine whether a company is under or overvalued. If the company has a low market to book ratio, it is most likely undervalued and could be considered a good investment opportunity.

Example

ABC Company has a share price of $6.15 at the end of the year and a book value per share of $5.20 also at the end of the year. This gives a market to book ratio of 1.18. This means that the company is overvalued and that the investors are willing to pay a premium to purchase the shares. A market to book ratio of less than 1 could indicate that the company is undervalued.

$$\text{Market to book} = \frac{6.15}{5.20} = 1.18$$

Note

Market to book ratio is also known as price to book ratio.

Market to debt ratio

Type: Market value measure

Formula

$$\text{Market to debt} = \frac{\text{Total liabilities}}{\text{Total liabilities} + \text{Market value of equity}}$$

Description

The *market to debt ratio* is used to determine the financial strength of a company or to compare to other companies in a similar industry. A higher ratio means that the company has more debt compared to its market value of equity. A similar ratio, debt to capital, uses book value of equity for the same purpose.

Example

ABC has total liabilities in the amount of $79,930 and market value of equity in the amount of $61,500. This gives a market to debt ratio of 0.57.

$$\text{Market to debt} = \frac{79,930}{79,930 + 61,500} = 0.57$$

Market value added (MVA)

Type: Market value measure

Formula

$$\text{Market value added}\,(\text{MVA}) = \text{Market value} - \text{Invested capital}$$

Description

The *market value added* shows the difference between the market value (market cap) of a company and the capital contributed by investors (total common equity). The higher the market value added, the more value a company has created for shareholders. Should this number be negative, it means that investor capital has been destroyed.

Example

ABC Company has a market cap of $61,000 and invested capital in the amount of $52,070. This gives a market value added of $9,430.

$$\text{Market value added}\,(\text{MVA}) = 61,500 - 52,070 = 9,430$$

Thus, ABC has created $9,430 in value for its investors above the capital they have invested.

Note

Market value added differs from economic value added (EVA). Market value added is a market value measure whereas economic value added is a performance measure, measuring the company's true profitability.

Market value of equity

Type: Market value measure

Formula

Market value of equity = Stock price × Number of shares outstanding

Description

The *market value of equity*, also known as market cap, is the total market value of a company's outstanding shares. Market value of equity is calculated by multiplying the company's shares outstanding by the current share price. Investors often use the market value of equity to determine a company's size, as opposed to sales or total asset figures.

Example

ABC Company has a stock price of $6.15 per share at December 31, 2013, and 10,000 of shares outstanding. This gives a market value of equity of $61,500.

$$\text{Market value of equity} = 6.15 \times 10,000 = 61,500$$

Note

Market value of equity is also known as market capitalization or market cap.

Net cash flow

Type: Cash flow measure

Formula

$$\text{Net cash flow} = \text{Net income} + \text{Depreciation} + \text{Amortization}$$

Description

The *net cash flow* is the sum of net income plus noncash expenses such as depreciation and amortization. Net cash flow shows the true cash generated by the company.

Example

ABC Company has net income in the amount of $9,475, depreciation and amortization in the amount of $37 and $100, respectively. This gives ABC Company a net cash flow in the amount of $9,950.

$$\text{Net cash flow} = 9,475 + 357 + 100 = 9,950$$

Net cash flow can be used to judge the amount of cash a company truly has to tap in order to invest in future growth or return to shareholders.

Net operating profit after taxes (NOPAT)

Type: Performance measure

Formula

$$NOPAT = EBIT \times (1 - Tax\ rate)$$

Description

The *net operating profit after taxes* measures what the company's earnings would have been if the company had no debt and no financial assets that produce interest expenses and interest income, respectively.

Example

ABC Company has EBIT in the amount of $13,525 and an effective tax rate of 23.86%. This amounts NOPAT of $10,298.

$$NOPAT = 13,525 \times (1 - 02386) = 10,298$$

NOPAT is a useful performance measure and a better indicator than net income when comparing companies' operations against one another. NOPAT does not take into consideration the debt structure of the company nor its financial assets.

Note

NOPAT is used in the calculation of operating cash flow.

Net operating working capital (NOWC)

Type: Performance measure

Formula

NOWC = Operating current assets − Operating current liabilities

Description

The *net operating working capital* measures the company's liquidity and potential for growth. Net operating working capital is equal to cash, accounts receivables, and inventories less accounts payable and accruals. Operating current assets are defined as cash, receivables, and inventories. Operating current liabilities are defined as accounts payable and accruals.

Example

ABC Company has operating current assets in the amount of $69,355 and operating current liabilities in the amount of $46,110. This gives the company net operating working capital (NOWC) of $46,110.

$$NOWC = 69,355 - 23,245 = 46,110$$

Net profit margin

Type: Profitability measure

Formula

$$\text{Net profit margin} = \frac{\text{Net income}}{\text{Sales}}$$

Description

The *net profit margin* formula looks at how much of a company's revenues are kept as net income. The net profit margin is generally expressed as a percentage. Both net income and sales can be found on a company's income statement.

Example

ABC Company has net income in the amount of $9,475 and total sales in the amount of $210,000. This gives a net profit margin of 4.51%, which means that for every $100 of sales, $4.51 of net income is generated.

$$\text{Net profit margin} = \frac{9,475}{210,000} = 4.51\%$$

Note

In some cases, in a mature market a decline in the company's profit margin can represent a price war, which is lowering profits. A decline in profit margins can also be a pricing strategy in order for the company to increase its market share.

Operating cash flow (OCF)

Type: Cash flow measure

Formula

$$\text{Operating cash flow} = \text{NOPAT} + \text{Depreciation} + \text{Amortization}$$

Description

The operating cash flow is the cash generated by the company's everyday business operations. It is used to determine the amount of cash normal operations are generating to see whether or not outside cash will be required to grow the company.

Example

ABC Company has NOPAT in the amount of $10,298, depreciation in the amount of $375, and amortization in the amount of $100. This gives the company operating cash flow (OCF) in the amount of $10,773.

$$\text{Operating cash flow} = 10{,}298 + 357 + 100 = \$10{,}773$$

Thus, if ABC Company determined that it would need $15 million to grow the business to the next level, they would have some sense of how much outside cash would be needed (approximately $4.23 million).

Operating profit margin

Type: Performance measure

Formula

$$\text{Operating profit margin} = \frac{\text{EBIT}}{\text{Sales}}$$

Description

The *operating profit margin* is a measurement of what proportion of a company's revenue is left over after paying for variable costs of production such as wages, raw materials, and so on. A healthy operating margin is required for a company to be able to cover other costs such as depreciation, interest expenses, profit to shareholders, and profit to invest in the growth of the company. Another way to look at it is that operating profit margin tells you how good the company is at generating profits from its core business, as opposed to all other aspects of the company.

Example

ABC Company has earnings before interest and taxes (EBIT) in the amount of $13,525 and sales in the amount of $210,000. This gives an operating profit margin of 6.44%.

$$\text{Operating profit margin} = \frac{13,525}{210,000} = 6.44\%$$

An operating profit margin of 6.44% means that for every $100 of sales, the company generates $6.44 of EBIT. This can be compared to other companies in the industry to see how good the company is at generating profits from their core business, instead of other means, and how much of the operating profit is eroded by other parts of the company.

Payable period (Days payable)

Type: Performance measure

Formula

$$\text{Payable period} = \frac{\text{Accounts payable}}{\text{Cost of sales} / 365}$$

Description

The *payable period* ratio, also known as days payable ratio, measures a company's average number of days between receiving goods and paying its suppliers for them. The greater the payable period, the greater number of days it takes the company to pay its suppliers.

Example

ABC Company has accounts payable in the amount of $18,460 and credit purchase per day in the amount of $163,000. This gives a payable period of 41.33 days.

$$\text{Payable period} = \frac{18,460}{163,000 / 365} = 41.33 \text{ days}$$

Payable period ratio of 41.33 means that the company pays its suppliers 41.33 days after receiving the products. The payable period is a reflection of the credit terms that are extended to the company by its supplier. In general, a ratio much higher than the industry average could mean that the company has liquidity problems and that the company is not paying its suppliers in a timely manner.

A decline in the payable period could be an indication of change in credit terms or an indication that the company has issues with its cash management. This number can be compared to the industry average, to other companies, or trended over time to see how a company is doing with payables. This number can also be compared to known payment terms to see if the company is paying on time.

Post-money valuation

Type: Valuation

Formula

$$\text{Post} - \text{money valuation} = \frac{\text{New investment amount}}{\text{New investment ownership}}$$

Description

The *post-money* (and pre-money) *valuation* are frequently used terms to describe the valuation of a company when raising capital. When a private equity firm, venture capitalist, or angel investor injects cash into a company in exchange for equity (ownership), the company's value immediately before the investment is called pre-money valuation, whereas the company's value immediately after the transaction is called post-money valuation.

Example

If a venture capital (VC) firm invests $10,000,000 for 25% equity in the company, then the post-money valuation would be equal to $40,000,000.

$$\text{Post} - \text{money valuation} = \frac{10,000,000}{25\%} = 40,000,000$$

Because the new investment amount in the company was $10,000,000, then the pre-money valuation is equal to $30,000,000.

$$\text{Pre} - \text{money valuation} = 40,000,000 - 10,000,000 = 30,000,000$$

Note

When raising capital, valuation and the dilution of ownership is an important issue for a business owner to understand. It is critical for the business owner to select the right partner as often venture capital brings business expertise and relationships in addition to capital.

Pre-money valuation

Type: Valuation measure

Formula

$$Pre - money\ valuation = Post\ money\ valuation - New\ investment$$

Description

The *pre-money* (and post-money) *valuation* are frequently used terms to describe the valuation of a company when raising capital. When a private equity firm, venture capitalist, or angel investor injects cash into a company in exchange for equity (ownership), the company's value immediately before the investment is called pre-money valuation, whereas the company's value immediately after the transaction is called post-money valuation.

Example

If a venture capital (VC) firm invests $10,000,000 for 25% equity in the company, then the post-money valuation would be equal to $40,000,000.

$$Post - money\ valuation = \frac{10,000,000}{25\%} = 40,000,000$$

Because the new investment amount in the company was $10,000,000, then the pre-money valuation is equal to $30,000,000.

$$Pre - money\ valuation = 40,000,000 - 10,000,000 = 30,000,000$$

Note

When raising capital, valuation and the dilution of ownership is an important issue for a business owner to understand. It is critical for the business owner to select the right partner as often venture capital brings business expertise and relationships in addition to capital.

Price earnings ratio (P/E ratio)

Type: Market value measure

Formula

$$P / E \text{ ratio} = \frac{\text{Price per share}}{\text{Earnings per share}}$$

Description

The *price earnings ratio* values the company's current share price compared to its per-share earnings. P/E ratios are one method for determining how "expensive" or "cheap" a stock is. When you are buying stock in a company, you are really buying the future earnings of that company. By dividing the price by the earnings gives you some sense of the value of the stock in comparable terms.

Example

ABC Company has a price per share in the amount of $6.15 and earnings per share in the amount of $9.48. This gives a P/E ratio of $6.49.

$$P / E \text{ ratio} = \frac{6.15}{9.48} = 6.49$$

This number can be compared to other companies in a similar industry. If one company has a substantially different P/E ratio than another, one can dig into details to find out if there is a reason for it. In some cases, the market has incorrectly valued a stock, offering the investor an arbitrage opportunity.

Price to book ratio

Type: Market value measure

Formula

$$\text{Price to book} = \frac{\text{Market price per share}}{\text{Book value per share}}$$

Description

The *price to book* ratio, also known as market to book ratio, measures the relative value of a company compared to its share price. The ratio can also be calculated as total market value over total book value as the per share part in the equation washes out.

Price to book ratio is a great tool to quickly determine whether a company is under or overvalued. If the company has a low price to book ratio, it is undervalued and considered a good investment opportunity.

Example

ABC Company has a share price of $6.15 at the end of the year and a book value per share of $5.20 also at the end of the year. This gives a price to book ratio of 1.18. This means that the company is overvalued and that the investors are willing to pay a premium to purchase the shares. A price to book ratio of less than 1 indicates that the company is undervalued.

$$\text{Price to book} = \frac{6.15}{5.20} = 1.18$$

Note

Price to book ratio is also known as market to book ratio.

Price to cash flow ratio

Type: Liquidity measure

Formula

$$\text{Price to cash flow} = \frac{\text{Price per share}}{\text{Cash flow per share}}$$

Description

The *price to cash flow ratio* shows the company's ability to generate cash and acts as an indicator of liquidity and solvency. Because accounting rules are different country by country, reported earnings and, therefore, price to earnings ratios, may not make a true comparison. Using cash flow per share is one method to strip away these differences.

Example

ABC Company has a price per share in the amount of $6.15 and cash flow per share in the amount of $0.81. This gives a price to cash flow ratio of $7.55.

$$\text{Price to cash flow} = \frac{6.15}{0.8145} = 7.55$$

This number can be compared to other companies in a similar industry.

Price to sale ratio

Type: Market value measure

Formula

$$\text{Price to sale} = \frac{\text{Price per share}}{\text{Revenue per share}}$$

Description

The *price to sale ratio* is a market value measure, typically used in the valuation of shares. Price to sale ratio is calculated as price per share divided by revenue per share.

Example

ABC Company has a price per share at the end of the year in the amount of $6.10 and revenue per share in the amount of $21.00. This gives a price to sale ratio of 29.28%.

$$\text{Price to sale} = \frac{6.15}{21.00} = 29.28\%$$

Price to sale ratio can also be calculated as market capitalization divided by total sales.

$$\text{Price to sale} = \frac{\text{Market Cap}}{\text{Total Sales}} = \frac{61,500}{210,000} = 29.28\%$$

The price to sale can vary significantly by industry and should therefore only be trended over time or compared to other companies in a similar industry.

Profit margin

Type: Profitability measure

Formula

$$\text{Profit margin} = \frac{\text{Net income}}{\text{Sales}}$$

Description

The *profit margin* also known as net profit margin, measures how much of every dollar of sales a company keeps in earnings.

Example

ABC Company has net income in the amount of 9,475 and sales in the amount of 210,000. This gives a profit margin of 4.51%.

$$\text{Profit margin} = \frac{9,475}{210,000} = 4.51\%$$

A profit margin of 4.50% means that the company earns \$4.5 for every \$100 of sales. A declining profit margin can be an indication of price pressure from competitors, higher cost of sales, change in product mix, or higher operating cost.

Note

A decline in the company's profit margin can in some cases in a mature market represent a price war, which is lowering profits. A decline in profit margins can also be a pricing strategy in order for the company to increase its market share.

Quick ratio (Acid test)

Type: Liquidity measure

Formula

$$\text{Quick ratio} = \frac{\text{Current assets} - \text{Inventory}}{\text{Current liabilities}}$$

Description

The *quick ratio* shows whether a company has enough short-term assets to cover its immediate liabilities without selling inventory. The higher the quick ratio, the safer a position the company is in.

Example

ABC Company has currents assets in the amount of $69,765, inventory in the amount of $24,875, and current liabilities in the amount of $28,500. This gives a quick ratio of 1.58, which indicates that the company has sufficient current assets to cover its current liabilities more than one and a half times over without selling inventory.

$$\text{Quick ratio} = \frac{69,765 - 24,875}{28,500} = 1.58$$

The quick ratio is very similar to the current ratio except that it excludes inventory because inventory is often illiquid. The nature of the inventory will determine if the acid test or the current ratio is more applicable to your situation.

Note

The quick ratio is also known as the acid test.

Receivable turnover

Type: Performance measure

Formula

$$\text{Receivable turnover} = \frac{\text{Sales}}{\text{Receivable}}$$

Description

The *receivable turnover* measures the number of times receivables are converted into cash in a given period. This is different from the average collection period which shows the number of days it takes to collect the receivables.

Ideally, credit sales should be used in the numerator and average receivables in the denominator. However, these figures are often not readily available in the financial statements.

Example

ABC Company has sales in the amount of $210,000 and receivable in the amount of $28,030. This gives a receivable turnover ratio of 7.49. The higher the receivable turnover ratio is, the better the company is at converting receivables into cash. A decline in the turnover ratio could mean either a decline in sales or an indication that the customers are taking a longer time to pay for their purchases.

$$\text{Receivable turnover} = \frac{210,000}{28,030} = 7.49$$

The company can improve the turnover ratio by many methods. The most popular approach is offering a discount to the customers that pay their outstanding balance earlier, for example, within 30 days of the sales.

Note

Receivable turnover is also known as the accounts receivable turnover.

Receivable collection period

Type: Performance measure

Formula

$$\text{Receivable collection period} = \frac{\text{Days} \times \text{Account receivable}}{\text{Credit sales}}$$

Description

The *receivable collection period* indicates the amount of time (in days) it takes a company to convert its receivables into cash.

Example

ABC Company has accounts receivable in the amount of $28,030 and credit sales in the amount of $210,000. (In this example, credit sales and total sales are identical.) This gives a receivable collection period of 48.72 days, which means that it takes a little over one and a half month for the company to convert credit sales into cash.

$$\text{Receivable collection period} = \frac{365 \times 28,030}{210,000} = 48.72 \text{ days}$$

The company's credit terms will have a significant impact on the average collection period. The better the credit terms, the higher the average collection period. An increase in the receivable collection period could indicate increased risk of the company's customers not being able to pay for their purchases. A possible result is that the company will have to reserve for potential losses or expense bad debt. Most large companies (nonretail) do not handle many cash sales. Therefore, when looking at financial statements, it can be assumed that total sales do not include any cash sales. However, in smaller companies and in retail businesses, cash sales can be a significant part of the total sales.

Note

The receivable collection period is also known as the average collection period or simply collection period.

Return on equity (ROE)

Type: Profitability measure

Formula

$$\text{Return on equity} = \frac{\text{Net income}}{\text{Shareholder's equity}}$$

Description

The *return on equity* is the amount of net income generated as a percentage of shareholders equity. If the whole concept of business in general is dominated by the idea that you can take some money and turn it into more money, then return on equity is the king of all ratios. ROE measures the company's profitability by how much profit is generated with the money shareholders have invested.

Example

ABC Company has net income in the amount of $9,475 and shareholders' equity in the amount of $52,070. This gives a return on equity (ROE) of 18.19%, which means that for every $100 of equity the company generates $18.19 of net income.

$$\text{Return on equity} = \frac{9,475}{52,070} = 18.19\%$$

ROE is a valuable number both on its own and compared to other companies. Ideally, you will invest in companies with the highest ROE. All companies strive to make ROE higher. See the DuPont formula for a breakdown of ROE into its component to better understand the full picture of how a company generates ROE.

Return on assets (ROA)

Type: Profitability measure

Formula

$$\text{Return on assets} = \frac{\text{Net income}}{\text{Total assets}}$$

Description

The *return on assets* shows how profitable a company's assets are in generating revenue, that is, a ratio of 25% means that for every $100 of investment in assets, net income of $25 is generated.

Example

ABC Company has net income in the amount of $9,475 and total assets in the amount of $132,000. This gives an ROA of 7.18%. This means that for every $100 of investment in assets the company generates $7.18 of net income.

$$\text{Return on assets} = \frac{9,475}{132,000} = 7.18\%$$

ROA can also be calculated by multiplying the profit margin by the total asset turnover.

$$\text{Return on assets} = \text{Profit Margin} \times \text{Asset Turnover}$$

$$\text{Return on assets} = 4.51 \times 1.59 = 7.18\%$$

Return on capital (ROC)

Type: Profitability measure

Formula

$$\text{Return on capital} \left(\text{ROC}\right) = \frac{\text{Net income} - \text{Dividend}}{\text{Invested capital}}$$

Description

The *return on capital*, also known as return on invested capital (ROIC), measures a company's efficiency in allocating capital under its control to profitable investments.

When the ROC is greater than the cost of capital (WACC), the company is creating shareholder value; when it is less than the cost of capital, shareholder value is destroyed as the company grows. This is one case in which sales growth is not always desirable!

Example

ABC Company has net income in the amount of $9,475, dividend payout in the amount of $3,000, and total invested capital in the amount of $52,070. This gives an ROC in the amount of 12.44%.

$$\text{Return on Capital} \left(\text{ROC}\right) = \frac{9,475 - 3,000}{52,070} = 12.44\%$$

Note

Return on capital (ROC) is also known as return on invested capital (ROIC).

Return on invested capital (ROIC)

Type: Profitability measure

Formula

$$\text{Return on invested capital}\left(\text{ROIC}\right) = \frac{\text{Net income} - \text{Dividend}}{\text{Invested capital}}$$

Description

The *return on invested capital,* also known as return on capital (ROC), measures a company's efficiency in allocating capital under its control to profitable investments.

When the ROC is greater than the cost of capital (WACC), the company is creating shareholder value; when it is less than the cost of capital, shareholder value is destroyed as the company grows.

Example

ABC Company has net income in the amount of $9,475, dividend payout in the amount of $3,000, and total invested capital in the amount of $52,070. This gives a return on capital (ROC) in the amount of 12.44%.

$$\text{Return on invested capital}\left(\text{ROIC}\right) = \frac{9,475 - 3,000}{52,070} = 12.44\%$$

Note

Return on invested capital (ROIC) is also known as return on capital (ROC).

Return on investment (ROI)

Type: Profitability measure

Formula

$$ROI = \frac{\text{Gain from investment} - \text{Cost of investment}}{\text{Cost of investment}}$$

Description

The *return on investment* measures the efficiency of an investment and can also be used to compare a number of past or prospective investments.

Example

ABC Company considers investing in one additional production unit. The cost of the new unit is $4,650 and is estimated to produce cash inflows in the amount of $5,520 over a three-year period. The ROI for the company for this specific investment is 18.71%.

$$ROI = \frac{5,520 - 4,650}{4,650} = 18.71\%$$

This number can be compared to other investment options and nonfinancial factors to make business decisions.

Note

This calculation does not take into account the time value of money. For further discussion on investment and capital allocation, see Part Four – Capital Allocation at the end of this book.

Return on net assets (RONA)

Type: Profitability measure

Formula

$$RONA = \frac{\text{Net income}}{\text{Fixed assets} + \text{Working capital}}$$

Description

The *return on net assets* is a measure of the financial performance of the company that relates earnings to the company's assets that generate earnings; fixed assets such as equipment and property, and working capital. The higher the ratio, the better the company is at efficiently using its assets.

Example

ABC Company has net income in the amount of $9,475 and fixed assets plus working capital in the amount of $73,885. This gives a RONA of 12.83%. This means that for every $100 of investment in net assets the company generates $12.83 of net income.

$$RONA = \frac{9,475}{32,620 + 41,265} = 12.83\%$$

RONA is a valuable number both on its own and compared to other companies. Ideally, you would invest in companies with the highest RONA.

Return on sales (ROS)

Type: Profitability measure

Formula

$$\text{Return on sales} \left(\text{ROS}\right) = \frac{\text{EBIT}}{\text{Net sales}}$$

Description

The *return on sales* shows the company's operational efficiency. ROS is also known as the company's operating profit margin or the margin before interest (which can vary by company based on capitalization) and taxes (which also vary by company).

Example

ABC Company has earnings before interest and taxes (EBIT) in the amount of $13,525 and net sales in the amount of $210,000. This gives a return of sales (ROS) of 6.44%. This means that for every $100 of sales, the company generates $6.44 of EBIT.

$$\text{Return on sales} \left(\text{ROS}\right) = \frac{13,525}{210,000} = 6.44\%$$

This number can be compared to the industry average or to other companies to see how a company is performing relative to its peers.

Revenue per employee

Type: Performance measure

Formula

$$\text{Revenue per employee} = \frac{\text{Sales}}{\text{Number of employee}}$$

Description

The *revenue per employee* shows the company's sales in relation to its number of employees.

Example

ABC Company has sales in the amount of $210,000 and the total number of employees of 875. This gives revenue per employee in the amount of $240. This means that on average each employee generates $240 of sales.

$$\text{Revenue per employee} = \frac{210,000}{875} = 240$$

A company can use this ratio to compare itself to other companies in the same industry. A company wants the highest revenue per employee possible, everything else equal, as it denotes higher productivity.

Note

Comparing one company's revenue per employee to another usually tells you as much about their industries as it tells you about the specific companies. The revenue per employee ratios generally tend to be lower in consulting and services companies compared to manufacturing companies in other industries that have invested significantly in fixed assets.

Pipeline, mining, and energy are some of the industries with the highest revenue per employee. At the other end of the spectrum are companies in the consulting and food and service industry.

Rule of 72

Type: Other

Formula

$$\text{Rule of } 72 = \frac{72}{\text{Interest rate}}$$

Description

The *rule of 72* shows the approximate number of years that it takes to double an investment at a given interest rate, by dividing the interest rate into 72.

Example

ABC Company has an investment in the amount of $100,000 that yields 12% return every year. Using the rule of 72, it will then take approximately six years for the investment to reach a balance of $200,000.

$$\text{Rule of } 72 = \frac{72}{12} = 6$$

As illustrated in this Excel table, the rule of 72 is only an approximation of the time it takes to double an investment at a given interest rate.

A	B	C	D	F	G
1					
2	Year	Principal	Interest 12%	Balance	
3	1	100,000	12,000	112,000	
4	2	112,000	13,440	125,440	
5	3	125,440	15,053	140,493	
6	4	140,493	16,859	157,352	
7	5	157,352	18,882	176,234	
8	6	176,234	21,148	197,382	
9	7	197,382	23,686	221,068	
10					

Sustainable growth rate (SGR)

Type: Debt measure

Formula

$$\text{Sustainable growth rate} = \text{ROE} \times \left(1 - \text{dividend payout ratio}\right)$$

Description

The *sustainable growth rate* measures the maximum growth rate the company can sustain without changing its capital structure, for example, having to increase its financial leverage or issuing equity. In this case, the terminology should really be "self-sustainable" as the sustainable growth rate is the maximum rate a company can grow without going to outside sources for capital.

Example

ABC Company has a return on equity of 18% and a dividend payout ratio of 31.57%. Using the SGR, this gives a sustainable growth rate of 12.32%.

$$\text{Sustainable Growth Rate} = 0.18 \times \left(1 - 0.3157\right) = 12.32\%$$

This means that the maximum increase in sales that the company can sustain without changing its capital structure is from $210,000 in 2013 to $235,872 in 2014—an increase of 12.32%. If the company wishes to pursue growth in excess of this, it will have to seek outside capital.

Terminal value (Horizon value)

Type: Other

Formula

$$\text{Terminal value} = \frac{\text{FCF} \times (1 + \text{growth rate})}{\text{WACC} - \text{growth rate}}$$

Description

The *terminal value*, also known as the horizon value, shows the value of future operations beyond the end of the forecast period. It is calculated as the present value of all future cash flows after the forecast period, which is the period in which the company expects a constant growth rate in perpetuity. Terminal value is often used in valuation models for the period beyond which you don't have specific financial data but expect the company to grow at some constant rate.

Example

ABC Company has free cash flow in the amount of $5,360, WACC in the amount of 8.4%, and an assumed constant growth rate of 3%. This gives a terminal value in the amount of $102,237.

$$\text{Terminal value} = \frac{5,360 \times (1 + 0.03)}{8.4\% - 3.0\%} = 102,237$$

Note

The terminal value is also known as the horizon value.

Times interest earned (TIE)

Type: Debt measure

Formula

$$\text{Times interest earned} = \frac{\text{EBIT}}{\text{Interest expense}}$$

Description

The *times interest earned,* also known as interest coverage, measures a company's ability to pay interest on its outstanding debt and to what extent operating income can decline before the company is unable to meet its annual interest expenses.

The lower the ratio, the higher the likelihood that the company will not be able to service its debt (pay interest expenses on its debt). If the TIE ratio goes below 1, the company is not generating enough earnings to service its debt.

Example

ABC Company has earnings before interest and taxes (EBIT) in the amount of $13,525 and interest expenses in the amount of $1,190. This gives a TIE ratio in the amount of 11.37, which means that the company has earnings more than 11 times its interest expense.

$$\text{Times interest earned} = \frac{13,525}{1,190} = 11.37$$

A TIE ratio of 11.37 provides sufficient coverage that the company will be able to service its debt.

Note

Times interest earned is also known as interest coverage.

Total assets turnover

Type: Performance measure

Formula

$$\text{Total assets turnover} = \frac{\text{Sales}}{\text{Total assets}}$$

Description

The *total assets turnover* ratio measures the sales generated per dollar of assets and is an indication of how efficient the company is in utilizing their assets to generate sales.

Asset-intensive companies such as mining, manufacturing, and so on will generally have lower asset turnover ratios compared to companies that have fewer assets such as consulting and service companies.

Example

ABC Company has sales in the amount of $210,000 and total assets in the amount of $132,000. This gives a total asset turnover ratio of 1.59.

$$\text{Total asset turnover} = \frac{210,000}{132,000} = 1.59$$

This means that for every dollar invested in assets the company generates $1.59 of sales. This number should be compared to the industry average for companies in the same industry.

WACC (Weighted average cost of capital)

Type: Other

Formula

$$WACC = W_d \times R_d \times (1 - Tax\ rate) + W_{ps} \times R_{ps} + W_{cs} \times R_{cs}$$

Description

WACC means *weighted average cost of capital*, also known as cost of capital, and measures the company's average costs of financing. Most companies are financed by both debt and equity.

WACC measures the weighted average cost of these two sources of capital. This rate is most often used in capital allocation for evaluating future projects. In general, all projects that the company takes on should yield a return greater that the weighted average cost of capital.

Example

ABC Company has total debt in the amount of $79,930. The weight of the company's financing is 61% debt and 39% equity, the rate of which is financed with 7% and 13%, respectively. The company's effective tax rate is 22%. Tax rate used in the calculation should be the company's effective tax rate and not the statutory rate.

This gives a weighted average cost of capital in the amount of 8.40%. Projects that are not expected to return greater than 8.40% would generally be declined unless they show some other noneconomic benefit to the company.

$$WACC = 0.61 \times 0.07 \times (1 - 0.22) + 0 \times 0 + 0.39 \times 0.13 = 8.40\%$$

W_d, W_{ps}, and W_{cs} are the weights (percentages) used for debt, preferred and common shares, respectively. R_d, R_{ps}, and R_{cs} are the (interest) rates for debt, preferred, and common shares. Note that ABC Company has no preferred shares, respectively.

Weighted average cost of capital (WACC)

Type: Other

Formula

$$WACC = W_d \times R_d \times (1 - \text{Tax rate}) + W_{ps} \times R_{ps} + W_{cs} \times R_{cs}$$

Description

The *weighted average cost of capital,* also known as cost of capital or WACC, measures the company's average costs of financing. Most companies are financed by both debt and equity.

WACC measures the weighted average cost of these two sources of capital. This rate is most often used in capital allocation for evaluating future projects. In general, all projects that the company takes on should yield a return greater that the weighted average cost of capital.

Example

ABC Company has total debt in the amount of $79,930. The weight of the company's financing is 61% debt and 39% equity, the rate of which is financed with 7% and 13%, respectively. The company's effective tax rate is 22%. Tax rate used in the calculation should be the company's effective tax rate and not the statutory rate.

This gives a weighted average cost of capital in the amount of 8.40%. Projects that are not expected to return greater than 8.40% would generally be declined unless they show some other noneconomic benefit to the company.

$$WACC = 0.61 \times 0.07 \times (1 - 0.22) + 0 \times 0 + 0.39 \times 0.13 = 8.40\%$$

W_d, W_{ps}, and W_{cs} are the weights (percentages) used for debt, preferred and common shares, respectively. R_d, R_{ps}, and R_{cs} are the (interest) rates for debt, preferred, and common shares. Note that ABC Company has no preferred shares, respectively.

Working capital ratio

Type: Performance measure

Formula

$$\text{Working capital ratio} = \frac{\text{Current assets}}{\text{Current liabilities}}$$

Description

The *working capital* is the capital that a company has for day-to-day operations. The working capital ratio indicates whether the company has enough short-term assets (current assets) to cover its short-term liabilities (current liabilities) and thus leave the company with "working capital" to support its current operations. A ratio below 1 is an indication of negative working capital, meaning that the company will most likely not be able to cover its current short-term obligations.

Example

ABC Company has current assets in the amount of $67,765 and current liabilities in the amount of $28,500. This provides the company with a working capital ratio in the amount of $41,265 and a working capital ratio of 2.44.

$$\text{Working capital ratio} = \frac{69,765}{28,500} = 2.44$$

This means that the company can cover its short-term liabilities almost 2.5 times with its short-term assets. Companies may have a hurdle working capital ratio they need to meet in order to get funding from lenders.

Working capital is defined as current assets less current liabilities.

Working capital = Current assets − Current liabilities

Working capital = 69,765 − 28,500 = 41,265

ABC Company

The following section provides financial statement data for the hypothetical ABC Company, which are used to calculate most of the examples of financial ratios in this book.

This chapter includes the following financial statements by ABC Company:

- Income statement
- Balance sheet
  - Assets
  - Liabilities & equity
- Cash flow statements
- Supplementary information

It should be noted that these are not U.S. GAAP-compliant financial statements inasmuch as they include non-GAAP measures such as EBIT (earnings before interest and taxes) and EBITDA (earnings before interest, taxes, depreciation, and amortization).

In general, a non-GAAP financial measure is a measure of a company's performance, financial position, or cash flows that either excludes or includes amounts that are not normally excluded or included in the most directly comparable measure calculated and presented in accordance with GAAP (Generally Accepted Accounting Principles).

The following financial statements are structured to provide easy reference for the ratios in this book.

ABC Company—Income statement

ABC COMPANY—INCOME STATEMENT

(thousands of US dollars)

	2013	2012	2011
Sales	210,000	203,700	175,182
Cost of goods sold	(163,000)	(158,110)	(135,975)
Gross profit	47,000	45,590	39,207
Operating expenses (SG&A)	(33,000)	(32,010)	(27,529)
EBITDA	14,000	13,580	11,679
Depreciation	(100)	(97)	(83)
Amortization	(375)	(364)	(313)
EBIT	13,525	13,119	11,283
Interest income	110	107	92
Interest expense	(1,190)	(1,154)	(993)
Income before tax	12,445	12,072	10,382
Provision for tax	(2,970)	(2,881)	(2,478)
Net income	**9,475**	**9,191**	**7,904**
Retained earnings Jan 1	40,595	34,354	28,950
Net income	9,475	9,191	7,904
Dividend	(3,000)	(2,950)	(2,500)
Retained earnings Dec 31	**47,070**	**40,595**	**34,354**

COMPANY DATA	2013	2012	2011
Employees	875	847	840
Share price	$ 6.15	$ 6.20	$ 5.90
Dividend per share	$ 0.30	$ 0.30	$ 0.25
Effective tax rate	23.87%	23.87%	23.87%

ABC Company—Assets

ABC COMPANY—ASSETS

(thousands of US dollars)

	2013	2012	2011
Cash and cash equivalents	16,450	14,690	12,633
Securities	280	272	234
Accounts receivable	28,030	27,189	23,383
Inventory	24,875	24,882	21,399
Other current assets	130	126	108
Total current assets	**69,765**	**67,159**	**57,757**
Net PP&E	32,620	31,641	27,212
Other investments	8,740	8,478	7,291
Other long-term assets	20,875	20,249	17,414
Total non-current assets	**62,235**	**60,368**	**51,916**
Total Assets	**132,000**	**127,527**	**109,673**

ABC Company—Liabilities and equity

LIABILITIES AND SHAREHOLDERS' EQUITY

(thousands of US dollars)

	2013	2012	2011
Short term debt	2,795	2,711	2,332
Accounts payable	18,460	19,570	16,830
Accrued taxes	4,680	4,540	3,904
Other accruals	105	102	88
Current portion long-term debt	2,460	2,386	2,052
Total current liabilities	**28,500**	**29,309**	**25,206**
LT debt, less current portion	16,750	17,320	14,895
Deferred taxes	3,260	3,162	2,719
Other deferrals	29,820	30,589	26,307
Other long-term liabilities	1,600	1,552	1,192
Total non-current liabilities	**51,430**	**52,623**	**45,113**
Total liabilities	**79,930**	**81,932**	**70,319**
Common stock (10,000,000)	5,000	5,000	5,000
Retained earnings	47,070	40,595	34,354
Total shareholders equity	**52,070**	**45,595**	**39,354**
Total liabilities & equity	**132,000**	**127,527**	**134,879**

ABC Company—Cash flow statement
CASH FLOW STATEMENT
(thousands of US dollars)

	2013	2012	2011
Net income	9,475	9,191	7,904
Depreciation and Amortization	475	461	396
Change in receivable	(841)	(3,806)	(3,754)
Change in inventories	7	(3,483)	(2,875)
Change in other current assets	(4)	(18)	(22)
Change in account payable	(1,110)	2,740	2,258
Change in accruals	143	650	541
Operating activities	**8,145**	**5,735**	**4,448**
Cash used to acquire PP&E	(1,454)	(4,891)	(3,784)
Change in securities	(8)	(38)	(45)
Other long term liabilities	(626)	(1,187)	(1,254)
Change in short term investment	(262)	(2,835)	(2,258)
Investing activities	**(2,350)**	**(8,951)**	**(7,341)**
Change in debt	(412)	3,138	2,541
Deferred taxes & other deferrals	(623)	5,085	6,041
Dividend payment	(3,000)	(2,950)	(2,500)
Financing activities	**(4,035)**	**5,273**	**6,082**
Net change in cash	1,760	2,057	3,189
Cash at beginning of year	14,690	12,633	9,444
Cash at end of year	**16,450**	**14,690**	**12,633**

ABC Company—Supplementary information

SUPPLEMENTARY INFORMATION

(thousands of **US** dollars)

	2013	2012	2011
Cash and cash equivalents	16,450	14,690	12,633
Accounts receivable	28,030	27,189	23,383
Inventory	24,875	24,882	21,399
Operating current assets	**69,355**	**66,761**	**57,415**
Accounts payable	18,460	19,570	16,830
Accrued taxes	4,680	4,540	3,904
Other accruals	105	102	88
Operating current liabilities	**23,245**	**24,211**	**20,822**
Operating current assets	69,355	66,761	57,415
Operating current liabilities	23,245	24,211	20,822
Net operating working capital	**46,110**	**42,550**	**36,593**
Net operating working capital	46,110	42,550	36,593
Net PP&E	32,620	31,641	27,212
Other long-term assets	20,875	20,249	17,414
Total net operating capital	**99,605**	**94,440**	**81,218**
Short term debt	2,795	2,711	2,332
Current portion long-term debt	2,460	2,386	2,052
LT debt, less current portion	16,750	17,320	14,895
Total debt	**22,005**	**22,417**	**19,279**
Audit fees	200	190	175
Total professional services	**200**	**190**	**175**

4

Capital Allocation

Capital allocation is the process used to analyze projects and decide which ones should or should not be included in the company's *capital budget* (plan for spending money on growth and sustaining current operations). This chapter gives you the tools to make these decisions based upon potential growth and profitability. After the analysis has been performed, the capital budget itself outlines the planned expenditures on capital assets. The capital allocation process is important as it outlines the long-term investment strategy of the company.

The tools that we will describe in this chapter are:

- Net present value (NPV)
- Internal rate of return (IRR)
- Modified internal rate of return (MIRR)
- Payback method
- Discounted payback method
- Profitability index (PI)
- Total cost of ownership (TCO)

Large projects with high risk require more analysis. Smaller projects or replacement projects can often be analyzed by simply looking at the payback method or the internal rate of return.

These tools provide a variety of information to the key decision makers. By using Microsoft Excel it is very easy to set up the various formulas and compare each project's costs, benefits, and rates of return against those of others.

Net present value (NPV)

Description

The *net present value* (NPV) of a project is the present value of the future cash inflows less the present value of the future cash outflows discounted at the cost of capital (WACC). The higher the net present value, the more desirable it is to undertake the project.

Example

ABC Company considers investing in one additional production unit. The cost of the new unit is $4,650 and is estimated to produce net cash inflows in the amount of $5,520 over a three-year period. At the end of year three, the value of the production unit will be equal to zero.

The easiest way to calculate a projects NPV is to set up the year over year cash flows in Excel and use the Excel "=NPV" function to calculate the return as illustrated here:

	A	B	C	D	E	F	G
1							
2		Year	0	1	2	3	
3		Cash flows	(4,650)	1,100	1,850	2,570	
4							
5		NPV	=C3+NPV(F10,D3:F3)				
6							
7		Year	0	1	2	3	
8		Cash flows	(4,650)	1,100	1,850	2,570	
9							
10		NPV	296		WACC	5.00%	
11							

Based on the initial investment, the expected cash inflows, and the cost of capital of 5%, the new production unit will have an NPV of $296. This number can be compared to other projects to help determine a course of action with regard to capital allocation. At the very least, this number is positive and indicates that it is a worthwhile investment by itself, but perhaps not when compared to others or when considering the capital constrains of the company.

Internal rate of return (IRR)

Description

A project's *internal rate of return* (IRR) indicates the discount rate that makes the net present value of all cash in and out flows from the specific project equal zero under the assumption that the return can be reinvested at the same rate (the IRR rate). This number is not necessarily helpful to managers by itself, but only when compared to the IRR of other projects and to the company's WACC. The higher a project's internal rate of return, the more desirable it is to undertake the project.

Example

ABC Company considers investing in one additional production unit. The cost of the new unit is $4,650 and is estimated to produce net cash inflows in the amount of $5,520 over a three year period as laid out in the spreadsheet shown here. At the end of year three, the value of the production unit will be equal to zero. The easiest way to calculate a project's IRR is to set up the year over year cash flows in Excel and use the Excel "=IRR" function to calculate the return as illustrated here:

	A	B	C	D	E	F	G
1							
2		Year	0	1	2	3	
3		Cash flows	(4,650)	1,100	1,850	2,570	
4							
5		IRR	=IRR(C3:F3)				
6							
7		Year	0	1	2	3	
8		Cash flows	(4,650)	1,100	1,850	2,570	
9							
10		IRR	7.94%				
11							

Based on the expected cash flows, the new production unit will have an internal rate of return (IRR) of 7.94%. Again, this IRR alone tells you very little; it needs to be compared to other projects' IRRs and to the company's WACC in order to determine if the project should be pursued or not.

Modified internal rate of return (MIRR)

Description

Modified internal rate of return (MIRR) is no different than the internal rate of return (IRR) except that is assumes that the cash flows from the project are reinvested at the company's cost of capital (WACC) instead of the IRR. This makes MIRR a better indicator of the project's true benefit to the organization. The higher a project's modified internal rate of return, the more desirable it is to undertake the project.

Example

ABC Company considers investing in one additional production unit. The cost of the new unit is $4,650 and is estimated to produce net cash inflows in the amount of $5,520 over a three-year period as shown below. At the end of year three, the value of the production unit will be equal to zero.

The easiest way to calculate a projects MIRR is to set up the year over year cash flows in Excel and use the Excel "=MIRR" function to calculate the return as illustrated here:

	A	B	C	D	E	F	G
1							
2		Year	0	1	2	3	
3		Cash flows	(4,650)	1,100	1,850	2,570	
4							
5		MIRR	=MIRR(C3:F3,F10, F10)				
6							
7		Year	0	1	2	3	
8		Cash flows	(4,650)	1,100	1,850	2,570	
9							
10		MIRR	7.18%		WACC	5.00%	
11							

Based on the expected cash flows and a WACC of 5%, the new production unit will have MIRR of 7.18%. Again, the MIRR alone tells you very little; it needs to be compared to other projects MIRRs and to the company's WACC in order to determine if the project should be pursued or not.

Payback method

Description

The *payback method* measures the time it takes for a company to recover the capital invested in the project. The model does not consider the time value of money, nor does it consider the cash flows beyond the payback period. In general, the shorter the payback period, the more desirable it is to undertake the project. The payback method is usually considered a "quick and dirty" capital allocation tool given these simplifying assumptions.

Example

ABC Company considers investing in one additional production unit that costs $7,540 and is estimated to produce net cash inflows in the amount of $9,200 over a six-year period. Excel does not have a payback function but it can be calculated manually, by looking at the year where the cumulative cash flow becomes positive and dividing the cash flow from that year by the amount needed to become positive and adding it to that year.

	A	B	C	D	F
1					
2			Cash	Cumulative	
3		Year	Flow	Cash Flow	
4		0	(7,540)	(7,540)	
5		1	4,000	(3,540)	
6		2	3,000	(540)	←
7		3	1,000	460	
8		4	500	960	
9		5	400	1,360	
10		6	300	1,660	
11					
12		Payback period	=B6+(-D6/C7)		
13					
14		Payback period	2.54 years		
15					

Based on the expected cash flow, the payback period for the new production unit is 2.54 years.

Discounted Payback method

Description

The *discounted payback method* measures the time it takes for a company to recover the capital invested in the project. The discounted payback model takes into consideration the time value of money by discounting the cash flows at the cost of capital (WACC). This makes it a better indicator when compared to the regular payback method. In general, the shorter the discounted payback period, the more desirable it is to undertake the project.

Example

ABC Company considers investing in one additional production unit. The cost of the new unit is $7,540 and is estimated to produce cash inflows in the amount of $9,200 over a six-year period. There is no specific function in excel to calculate the discounted payback period. However, it can be calculated manually as outlined below, where the payback period is the period in which the cumulative cash flow becomes positive.

	A	B	C	D	F	G
1						
2				Discounted	Cumulative	
3		Year	Cash Flow	Cash Flow	Cash Flow	
4		0	(7,540)	(7,540)	(7,540)	
5		1	4,000	3,810	(3,730)	
6		2	3,000	2,721	(1,009)	
7		3	1,000	864	(146)	←
8		4	500	411	266	
9						
10		WACC		5%		
11						
12		Payback period		=B7+(-F7/D8)		
13						
14		Payback period		3.35	Years	
15						

Based on the expected cash flow and the cost of capital, the payback period for the new production unit is 3.35 years. This is slightly longer than the regular payback period as it takes into consideration the time value of money.

Profitability index

Description

The *profitability index* measures the relative profitability of a project calculated by dividing the present value of future cash flows of a project by the initial investment required for the project. The higher the profitability index, the more desirable it is to undertake the project. A value less than one indicate that the present value of the project is less that the initial investment and is therefore a bad investment.

ABC Company considers investing in one additional production unit. The cost of the new unit is $4,650 and is estimated to produce cash inflows in the amount of $5,520 over a three-year period. At the end of year three, the value of the production unit will be equal to zero. Discounting the future cash inflows at a discount rate of 5% (WACC) gives a present value of $4,946.

	A	B	C	D	E	F	G
1							
2		Year	0	1	2	3	
3		Cash flows	(4,650)	1,100	1,850	2,570	
4							
5		Investment	4,650	Invest amount			
6							
7		WACC	5%	Cost of capital			
8							
9		PV	4,946	PV of future cash flows			
10							
11		PI	1.06	Profitability index			
12							

Based on the initial investment, the expected future cash flow and the cost of capital of 5% the new production unit will have a Profitability index of 1.06 indicating that the present value of the future cash flow is larger than the initial investment.

Total cost of ownership (TCO)

Description

The tools discussed previously in this section are used to determine which projects should and should not be included in the capital budget. These tools often only highlight the direct benefits of the specific project under consideration. Good managers know that most projects do not exist in a vacuum and that there are often intangible benefits and drawbacks associated with new projects that modeling does not always include.

A *total-cost of ownership* (TCO) analysis can be used to measure the current and future contribution that a projects implementation adds to the company. Its focus is not solely on quantitative measures but also qualitative measures that include direct and indirect benefits.

Direct benefits are cash flows directly associated with the project. Indirect benefits include items such as overhead, operating and maintenance, productivity improvement, and so on.

Measuring qualitative benefits can be much harder as these are softer benefits, such as employee satisfaction, better work environment, resulting in less sick days, and so on. Some economists call these *social benefits*.

TCO analyses are typically done with large projects, such as a new ERP implementation or a new office building, to afford management an overview of all the costs and benefits associated with this new initiative before allocating capital to the specific project.

Completing a TCO analysis is quite comprehensive and time-consuming. The main reason is that qualitative data is not easy to quantify as is often generated by interviews, observations and comparison to similar projects either within the company or with similar companies in the industry. Total cost of ownership should therefore mainly be considered with larger projects or when qualitative benefits are significant to the quantities ones.

Abbreviations

AFN	Additional funds needed
BEP	Basic earnings power
CAGR	Compound annual growth rate
CAPM	Capital asset pricing model
CCC	Cash flow conversion cycle
CFROI	Cash flow return on investment
DPO	Days payable outstanding
DSO	Days sales outstanding
EBIT	Earnings before interest and taxes
EBITDA	EBIT plus depreciation and amoritization
EV	Enterprice value
EVA	Economic value added
FCF	Free cash flow
GAAP	Generally accepted accounting principles
IRR	Internal rate of return
MIRR	Modified internal rate of return
MVA	Market value added
NOPAT	Net operating profit after taxes
NOWC	Net operating working capital
NPV	Net present value

OCF	Operating cash flow
PE Ratio	Price to earnings ratio
PBIT	Profit before interest and taxes
PI	Profitability index
ROA	Return on assets
ROC	Return on capital
ROE	Return on equity
ROI	Return on investment
ROIC	Return on invested capital
RONA	Return on net assets
ROS	Return on sales
TCO	Total cost of ownership
TIE	Time interest earned
WACC	Weighted average cost of capital

Useful Websites

There are numerous websites where you can find additional information on financial ratios, financial information on public companies, and industry standards. Here are some of our favorites:

- www.aicpa.org
- www.barrons.com
- www.bloomberg.com
- www.businessweek.com
- www.cfo.com
- www.dealbook.nytimes.com
- www.fasb.org
- www.finance.yahoo.com
- www.hoovers.com
- www.investopedia.com
- www.marketwatch.com
- www.money.cnn.com
- www.morningstar.com
- www.online.barrons.com
- www.pehub.com
- www.reuters.com
- www.sec.gov
- www.wikipedia.org
- www.wsj.com

Index

Get the eBook for only $10!

Now you can take the weightless companion with you anywhere, anytime. Your purchase of this book entitles you to 3 electronic versions for only $10.

This Apress title will prove so indispensible that you'll want to carry it with you everywhere, which is why we are offering the eBook in 3 formats for only $10 if you have already purchased the print book.

Convenient and fully searchable, the PDF version enables you to easily find and copy code—or perform examples by quickly toggling between instructions and   applications. The MOBI format is ideal for your Kindle, while the ePUB can be utilized on a variety of mobile devices.

Go to www.apress.com/promo/tendollars to purchase your companion eBook.

Other Apress Business Titles You Will Find Useful

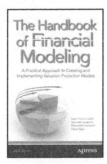

The Handbook of Financial Modeling
Avon
978-1-4302-6205-3

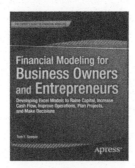

Financial Modeling for Business Owners and Entrepreneurs
Sawyer
978-1-4842-0371-2

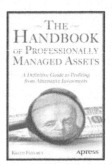

The Handbook of Professionally Managed Assets
Fevurly
978-1-4302-6019-6

Traders at Work
Bourquin/Mango
978-1-4302-4443-1

Practical Methods of Financial Engineering and Risk Management
Chatterjee
978-1-4302-6133-9

Tactical Trend Trading
Robbins
978-1-4302-4479-0

Broken Markets
Mellyn
978-1-4302-4221-5

Data Modeling of Financial Derivatives
Mamayev
978-1-4302-6589-4

Managing Derivatives Contracts
Shaik
978-1-4302-6274-9

Available at www.apress.com

Lightning Source UK Ltd.
Milton Keynes UK
UKOW04f0501050118

315532UK00001B/3/P